Date Due

NO

COMMUNICATION AND PERSUASION

Communication and Persuasion

G. H. Jamieson

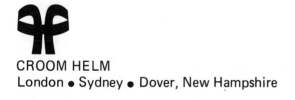

CROOM HELM
London • Sydney • Dover, New Hampshire

© 1985 G.H. Jamieson
Croom Helm Ltd, Provident House,
Burrell Row, Beckenham, Kent BR3 1AT

Croom Helm Australia Pty Ltd, First Floor,
139 King Street, Sydney, NSW 2001, Australia

British Library Cataloguing in Publication Data

Jamieson, G.H.
    Communication and persuasion. – (Croom
    Helm communication series)
    1. Persuasion (Psychology)
    I. Title
    302.2   BF637.P4

    ISBN 0-7099-1424-5

Croom Helm, 51 Washington Street,
Dover, New Hampshire 03820, USA

Library of Congress Cataloging in Publication Data

Jamieson, G.H. (G. Harry)
    Communication and persuasion.

    (The Croom Helm communication series)
    Includes bibliographies and index.
    1. Communication – Psychological aspects.
2. Persuasion (Psychology) 3. Learning, Psychology of.
I. Title. II. Series.
P96.P75J35 1985   001.51'01'9   84-23768
ISBN 0-7099-1424-5 (U.S.)

Printed and bound in Great Britain by
Biddles Ltd, Guildford and King's Lynn

CONTENTS

Contents

Contents

FIGURES

THE CROOM HELM COMMUNICATION SERIES

We are at the beginning of a communications revolut-
ion.

Developments in computers, electronic equipment and
telecommunications are bringing information technology to all aspects of work and leisure.

These developments are focusing our attention on
the storage, retrieval and use of information, the
way we communicate with others, with ourselves, and
with the world.

This series is intended to explore the many facets
of communication from those concerned with developments in information technology to those concerned
with all aspects of human communication.

This book COMMUNICATION AND PERSUASION is written
by Harry Jamieson, Head of the Department of Communication Studies at the University of Liverpool.
Persuasion is a factor ever present in our lives
whether we wish it or not. The press, television,
radio and a whole range of media are used as persuasive devices. This book is designed to explore
persuasion from a variety of viewpoints, from media
manipulation to the place of learning and resistance to persuasion. It will be of interest not only
to professional communicators and those concerned
in the pursuit of academic courses in communication
but also to all who are concerned with the quality
of life.

P.J. Hills,
Cambridge
February 1984.

PREFACE

In the western industrial society people are faced
with a range of media which are or can be used as
persuasive devices, the press, radio, television,
and street hoardings being familiar examples. Moreover, persuasion is an ever present factor in the
everyday lives of most people; for instance, even
during informal conversations between friends an
element of persuasion exists, when one or both of
the participants possesses convictions which they
desire to share.

The main intention of this book is to bring
to the attention of the reader the wider ramifications of persuasion; to show its sinews in the psychology of individuals, in the groups with whom
they connect, and in the wider field of society.
The topic is approached from the standpoint that
persuasion, in some form or other, is an inevitable
corollary to life; if value judgements are to be
made, then they will relate to the content, to the
degree or intensity of its application, to the methods employed, and to the ways in which control is
exercised over the media through which it finds its
outlet. But standing above all these issues is the
amount of freedom which the individual possesses, to
accept, reject, or even to display neutrality in the
presence of persuasive appeals.

In writing this book, the author is keenly aware
of a number of debts; first of all to his wife, Doris
for her patient help in many ways; to a long standing friend, Dr. Robert Cooper, for the subtle and
penetrating influence of his scholarship during many
years of good fellowship; to his former colleague,
Dr. Jon Baggaley, for his lively and spirited com-
panionship when working together at the Department
of Communication Studies at the University of Liverpool; to his present colleague, Mr. John Thompson;

to students past and present whose thoughts and
ideas have been a source of stimulation; to Miss
Vera Beckett for typing the initial draft; to Mrs
Doris Berry for typing the final draft; and, finally,
to Dr. Phil Hills for his encouragement.

ACKNOWLEDGEMENTS

Material from the following sources has been repro-
duced by kind permission of the publishers. Full
details of the citations appear in the references
which are given at the end of each chapter.

Baggaley, J. & Duck, S.:
    (1976) Dynamics of Television,(Gower).
Barthes, R.:
    (1973) Mythologies (Paladin) translated by
    Annette Lavers. First published in French by
    du Seuil in 1957, and in English by Jonathan
    Cape Ltd., in 1972.
Berlyne, D.E.:
    (1960) Conflict, Arousal & Curiosity,(McGraw-
    Hill).
Douglas, M.:
    (1973) Rules and Meanings, (Penguin).
Hill, W.F.:
    (1965) Learning,(Methuen).
Hinde, R.A.:
    (1972) Non-Verbal Communication,(Cambridge U.P.).
Hunter, I.M.L.:
    (1964) Memory, (Penguin).
Leech, G.:
    (1974) Semantics, (Penguin).
Pool, I.de Sola & Schramm, W.:
    (1973) Handbook of Communication, (Rand, McNally
    & Co.) Copyright (c) 1973 by Houghton Mifflin
    Company, Boston, U.S.A.
Sherif, C.W. & Sherif, M.:
    (1967) Attitude, Ego-Involvement and Change.
    (John Wiley).
Stevenson, C.L.:
    (1944) Ethics and Language, (Yale U.P.).

Acknowledgements

Wellman, C.:
    (1961) The Language of Ethics,(Harvard U.P.).
Wilden, A.:
    (1972) System and Structure, (Tavistock),

COMMUNICATION AND PERSUASION

INTRODUCTION

Interest in persuasion as a specialist field of
study is long standing, for example, in Graeco-Roman
times it held a special place in the educational cur-
riculum under the title of rhetoric which is still
a special area of study in some educational institutions. However, interest in persuasion has broad-
ened to include the impact of technological developments and there has been an expansion of interest
in face-to-face communication, a theme which we will
take up later when considering non-verbal effects.

This more general interest in persuasion has
been brought about by factors such as the advent of
compulsory education which brought in its train a
more literate society. The spread of literacy, the
introduction of the rotary press and quicker road
and rail transport brought about a massive rise in
circulation of the daily press. At the same time,
large-scale mass production of consumer goods created a need for national sales, and hence the expansion of commercial advertising, which used a variety
of media. Centralisation of the apparatus of the
state brought another agency, the government itself,
as a potential persuader, but here persuasion is
generally discussed in terms of propaganda rather
than advertising; a distinction often used in a pejorative sense.

Human communication often includes a substantial persuasive element. Natural language and its
accompanying non-verbal supports provide a ready-
made avenue for persuasion. In day-to-day activities persuasion is a normal accompaniment to behaviour; for instance, parents invariably attempt to
persuade their offspring to behave in ways which conform to their social milieu; teachers attempt to
persuade their students to accept particular standards. At the less personal level, advertisers

attempt to persuade people to buy their particular
products or services; governments attempt to secure,
via persuasion, the acceptance of certain guidelines,
or, in more authoritarian states, acceptance of the
ideological values of the regime.

The term persuasion is often tinged with negative overtones, hinting at manipulation. The popular literature on the subject tends also to have a
negative bias (e.g. Brown, 1963; Packard, 1962,1978;
and Sargant, 1957). Here ideas from behaviourism
and psychoanalysis are used for analysing the processes and techniques of persuasion. The setting
up of specialised departments of propaganda for the
purpose of strengthening the power of the state (the
prime example being Germany under National Socialism,
see Reimann, 1979) added a sinister note to the concept of persuasion. In order to avoid the slur attached to the term propaganda, the British Government
instituted, at that time, a department bearing the
title "Ministry of Information"; such a title could
be seen as a euphemism.

Any discussion on persuasion raises ethical
issues concerning the content of messages and their
form of presentation. Persuasion concerns real events in a particular social milieu, and in the minds
of individuals who evaluate and apportion emotive
judgements according to their particular moral standards. Persuasion in practice is not abstract, but
it can only be fully explored by abstracting for
study the variety of structures which lie at the
bases of human life; such bases are manifest in the
psyche of the individual, the social behaviour of
the individual, and the semiological means by which
man communicates within himself and with others.

Additionally we must consider intent. That
which is not intended, i.e. merely coincidental,
although it may produce effects, cannot be regarded
as persuasive in the sense that we shall employ that
word. Intention can be directed towards change in
beliefs, values, or actions; for example, a socratic
type of dialogue can be persuasive to participants
given to rational argument, where beliefs are subjected to scrutiny, while on the other hand, an
emotive, non-rational appeal can be more effective
with other people. In general, however, the intention of most persuasive appeals is to engender action,
action which is observable as a change in behaviour.

Furthermore, one cannot communicate content,
e.g. facts or ideas, without giving particular form
to the communication which can cause biases in the
recipients. For example, published details of a new

car model can provide technical information (content) and, at the same time, appear in an attractive way (form); the two factors, either separately or together, possess the potential to persuade, resulting in the purchase of the model on offer.

When considering persuasion, we need to envisage a spectrum, ranging from influence at the milder end, to coercion at the other stronger end. The midpoint is generally regarded as persuasive, implying a state between influence and coercion. Coercion is a condition of control not by voluntary acceptance of ideas, but more by fear of the consequences of non-compliance. Whereas it is generally acceptable to attempt to influence others by rational argument, coercion, except in certain institutional situations, for example prisons, is unacceptable. This leads to the concept of freedom. The move from open discussion between equals, to mediated communication, and then to coercion where behavioural control is exercised, is a move towards a restriction of freedom. In the mediated condition there is a restriction on argument, in the coercive situation there is a restriction on behaviour.

The study of persuasion can be seen from three distinct levels which provide a useful, if arbitrary, guide, namely (i) the individual as a psychological entity, (ii) the group, as a social and social-psychological factor, and (iii) society, as a political factor. There are, of course, mediating agencies which cross these boundaries, for example the verbal and non-verbal forms of communication which provide the core of persuasion, and the media of print, television etc.

Persuasion is conventionally discussed in the literature as bringing about changes in behaviour. However, it could be argued that persuasion may also be employed as a means for resisting change, as where people are persuaded to continue their existing allegiances, for example to continue the habit of purchasing a certain branded product, or continuing with an established voting pattern. This condition is appropriate to the model of a closed system, a homeostatic state, internally steady. The assumption here is that man has a built-in propensity to go 'off course' unless a corrective device is applied, the corrective device here being the persuasive message itself. Here we are touching upon the maintenance of the status quo in relation to larger systems which can be economic, political, or religious. Contemporary advertising offers examples which illustrate the potentiality of persuasion

to serve either function. The same tendency can be
seen in the appeals of political parties who canvass
support from the non-affiliated, but also canvass
for the continued allegiance of past supporters. However, persuasion, as previously stated, is sustained
by intention, that is intention to induce change or
intention to stem the possibility of change.

In many of the following chapters the concept
of relationship plays a critical role in the general
theme of persuasion. Sometimes this is made explicit, as for example in the chapters on learning and
signs, at other times it is implicit. The act of
persuasion often entails relating one thing to another: to a behaviour which brings a particular reward, or punishment; to what one is now to what one
can become. But these relationships always carry
a particular intention, an intention defined by the
persuader. Stripped of the intention aspect we can
see that persuasion theory shares common ground with
communication theory, as communication by its very
nature is centred upon the concept of relationships.
The work of Bateson (1973) at the biological level
and Cherry (1961) at the more mechanical level are
useful examples of this fact.

Persuasion may thus be considered a special
aspect of communication as it utilises various relationships that may be verbal or non-verbal, face-
to-face or spanning distance, via all the media at
man's disposal.

The framework of this book leads the reader to
consider persuasion as a force which operates upon
man in a personal sense, as a force which operates
upon the forms by which man communicates, and as a
force influencing man's interpersonal and societal
relationships.

REFERENCES

BATESON, G. (1973) Steps to an Ecology of Mind.
    St. Albans, Herts.: Paladin.
BROWN, J.A.C. (1963) Techniques of Persuasion.
    Harmondsworth: Penguin.
CHERRY, C. (1961) On Human Communication. New York:
    Science Editions; Wiley.
PACKARD, V. (1962) The Hidden Persuaders. Harmonds-
    worth: Penguin.
    "   (1978) The People Shapers. London:Futura.
REIMANN, V. (1979) The Man Who Created Hitler:
    Joseph Goebbels. London: Sphere Books.
SARGANT, W. (1957) Battle for the Mind. London:
    Heinemann.

Chapter One

THE PLACE OF LEARNING

When persuasion is studied at the level of the individual we can usefully borrow ideas stemming from the field of learning theory. As we shall see, learning and persuasion share common ground when the focus of attention is placed upon the change, modification, or reinforcement of human behaviour.

Learning is sometimes defined as the process through which some aspect of human behaviour (e.g. beliefs, attitudes or actions) is acquired or changed through an individual's encounter with events, mental or physical. Changes brought about through reflexive involuntary responses to stimuli are not usually regarded as learned responses.

The basis of learning is the establishment of relationships (associations or connections), which may be formed as the result of physical or mental activities. Learning is a correlative act, be it overt or covert, conscious or subconscious. Its constructive or reconstructive potential can be used for self-growth, but it provides an avenue for external influences.

In our appraisal of learning, we shall begin by referring to classical conditioned learning in the Pavlovian tradition. This will be followed by a more detailed explanation of stimulus-response learning theory in the Skinnerian tradition. These perspectives on learning provide an opportunity for considering persuasion in terms of controls exercised by (a) the environment, and (b) persons as controllers. Closed situations, e.g. prisons, schools, hospitals, where controls can be exercised and responses monitored, provide ideal situations for the application of these particular learning theories. To use the language of behaviour therapy, schedules and plans can be arranged for the purpose of eliciting desired responses (the desired responses are

those of the controllers). After considering these
behavioural theories, we shall turn our attention
to distance communication. In distance communication, provision of feedback to the message originator,
because it is mediated, is delayed, and in the case
of mass media it is usually non-existent. Advertising often falls into this category. In the first
place it may not even reach the desired audience,
and secondly, the advertiser is largely in the dark
about the effect of his message except when there
are clear signs linking the message to increased
sales. Of course, much of advertising is concerned
with goodwill, a 'commodity' which is hard to measure with any degree of accuracy.

Another important consideration for us to take
up is that of the internal cognitive state of the
recipients of information. Whatever the intention
of the sender, the thoughts of the receiver can
influence the response to the information, be it an
advertisement or a particular environmental situation.

S-R theories

For closed or captive situations where control can
be exercised with some precision over stimulus conditions and the rewards and punishments which can
be meted out, the study of persuasion can be approached in terms of stimulus-response learning theories. In coercive or dependency situations the individual can be subjected to a variety of controls
or persuasive influences which are intended to change his or her behaviour in a particular way or
direction. Life faces each of us with experiences
of this kind, usually intended to be benign. In the
upbringing of children, the child is invariably
faced with having to produce a desired form of behaviour, one that is socially acceptable in a particular milieu. Correct behaviour is often rewarded;
on the other hand, incorrect or undesirable behaviour may be punished, sometimes physically, sometimes verbally, and sometimes by the withholding of
a desired reward or pleasurable activity. Formal
school education generally displays the same characteristics of control, and the process is continued
into specific aspects of adult life whenever the
individual is in some form of dependency relationship, but here the controls may be less overtly noticeable.

In the psychological literature on learning,
the stimulus-response (S-R) tradition of learning is
of special value as a means of accounting for

persuasion which takes place in coercive situations, and, according to B.F. Skinner (1948: 1973), as a means for explaining behaviour in social life in general. Its main relevance to our theme is that of immediacy, in its original sense, defining the non-mediated situations where the individual is in face-to-face contact with events. In contrast, distance communication is always mediated, therefore it is less appropriate for consideration in terms of S-R learning.

In the following discussion we are concerned essentially with immediate situations, where communication tends to be situational, perceived through the various senses which pick up information from the environment.

Conditioned learning

Fears about manipulation expressed in twentieth century literature partially owe their origins to research into conditioned learning, sometimes referred to as classical or Pavlovian conditioning. In this tradition, cause and effect is discussed as a stimulus and response. And, as we shall see later, it shares a similar theoretical background to instrumental learning.

Conditioned learning relates to the pairing of dissimilar stimuli which come, after repeated presentation to elicit the same response. The example frequently given is of a dog salivating at the sound of a conditioned stimulus, a bell. In this example, salivation is said to be conditioned so that by a process of association, a transfer effect has taken place. The importance of this to a theory of persuasion lies in the 'triggering-off' of second-order, non-natural associations on the foundation of existing natural associations. However, Pavlov's original experiments were based on physiological evidence obtained in tightly controlled experimental situations, and it is rarely the case that human responses can be subjected to such fine degrees of control.

Schein et al (1961) writing on coercive persuasion put forward an interpretation in Pavlovian terms of the attempted indoctrination of American army prisoners in the hands of their Chinese captors at the time of the Korean war. They believed that once verbal behaviour consistent with the captor's ideology has been elicited and learned by being reinforced it could then be transferred to other cues or stimuli by a Pavlovian conditioning mechanism; thus behaviour initially elicited by a complex shaping process could be conditioned to a variety of

7

simple cues with which it has been paired.

In a general sense, advertisers can be seen to be attempting a form of conditioned learning when they associate brand names with natural situations; the implicit intention being the transfer of evoction from the natural to the unnatural (branded product). The weakness here, from a theoretical standpoint, is that the association is experienced at a mediated level, it thus misses the immediacy or sensory element as demonstrated in Pavlov's work; in other words, it is images which are presented, not natural events. However, mediated experiences can produce physiological effects, therefore, an association can still be made, although perhaps differing in intensity.

Instrumental learning

Instrumental learning, sometimes referred to as operant learning because of the emphasis which is placed on the operational responses elicited in the act of learning, is mainly associated with the work of B.F. Skinner (1938, 1948, 1953, 1973). His work is in the connectionist tradition pioneered by Thorndike (1931); but, whereas Thorndike did not preclude such concepts as attitude or purpose as contributory agents in learning, Skinner reserved no place for such mentalistic concepts in his work. It is important for any theory of persuasion to include mentalistic concepts as this places emphasis on conditions internal to the persuadee. To exclude such concepts places more emphasis on external, environmental factors that help to determine or to shape human behaviour. In Skinner's (1973, p.23) words, "The environment not only prods or lashes, it selects. Its role is similar to that in natural selection, though on a very different time scale, and was overlooked for the same reason. It is now clear that we must take into account what the environment does to an organism not only before but after it responds. Behaviour is shaped and maintained by its consequences. Once this fact is recognised we can formulate the interaction between organism and environment in a much more comprehensive way... Behaviour which operates upon the environment to produce consequences ('operant' behaviour) can be studied by arranging environments in which specific consequences are contingent upon it...The second result is practical. The environment can be manipulated."

So here we have an explicit statement of manipulation, but in fairness to Skinner, he appears not to see manipulation in sinister terms, but as a recognition that human life is one of contingencies. In his book Walden Two (1948) he describes an ideal society with benign intentions, but with individuals inevitably shaped or formed by the rules and conditions of their surroundings. If we accept that Skinner's formulation regarding human behaviour is valid, then important implications would follow for theory building in persuasion.ゝ For example, the persuader is the controller specifying environmental conditions in which the persuadee would need to make appropriate responses in order to achieve outcomes satisfying to both himself and the controller. Such a condition would appear to have a greater element of feasibility in closed or captive situations where the respondent is in some form of dependency relationship. Schein et al(1961) discussed the theoretical implications in relation to prisoners of war, and Packard (1978) cited a wide variety of instances of attempted behaviour modification in line with Skinner's principles of behaviour, from school classrooms to control over sexual deviancy. Packard's work is couched in journalistic terms, but he points out that the use of conditioning techniques in a free society is still more of an aim than an achieved fact. Skinner's point of view is that all societies in all places and at all times, irrespective of ideological differences, inevitably condition their members, that it is not an argument about conditioning people, but about the best way of arranging the environment and the contingencies produced therein in order to bring about 'desirable' behaviour.

Packard, reviewing work in the field of conditioning, gave a number of conditions for its successful effects as envisaged by controllers, the most important being the nature of the institution. Closed situations, such as hospitals, schools, and prisons were the most effective. However, the permanency of the effects is open to question; in many cases, subjects have shown relapses a short time after leaving the experimental situation. Schein's finding that returning prisoners from the Korean war, who had been subjected to planned indoctrination, with few exceptions reverted to their initial beliefs, supports the experimental evidence. However, this reversal (i.e. change) in behaviour could be attributed to the contingencies in the new situation rather than to relapse.

Central to Skinner's work is that of reinforcement (i.e. the strengthening of relationships between stimuli and response). Reinforcement is related to a person's own responses, but the type of rein-

forcement, whether it be rewarding (positive reinforcement) or punishing (negative reinforcement)
can be in the power of an external agency, a controller. Control over the process of conditioning
in instrumental learning can take two main directions:
(i) variation in the rate of presentation of reinforcement; and (ii) variation in the time of presentation of reinforcement. In terms of planning,
the process can be scheduled, and this is of considerable interest in the construction of a theory
of persuasion. Let us take a closer look at the
effects of the various combinations of schedules of
reinforcement. According to Hill (1965) the simpl-
est schedule is continuous reinforcement where for
every response the recipient makes a reinforcement
is given, positive when correct, and negative when
wrong; an appropriate schedule when a person is unfamiliar with the situation. When the correct responses are made the schedule may be modified to what
is known as intermittent reinforcement; in this situation, only some of the responses are followed by
reinforcement. This is a highly manipulative view
of behavioural control, in which the thoughts of the
recipient are neither discussed or taken into consideration, it is the responses that matter.

How do these schedules of reinforcement differ,
if at all, in their effect? According to Hill (1965)
more responses are likely on any kind of intermittent schedule than on continuous reinforcement; also,
the likelihood of the newly shaped behaviour persis-
ting is greater after the intermittent type of reinforcement. We can speculate that the element of
uncertainty in intermittent reinforcement sustains
attention at a higher level, it has greater arousal value. But this only applies when correct responses have been previously established.

We might ask, what is the persuasive element in
this process? It is, in fact, the process itself.
The recipient is coerced into producing a certain
form of behaviour on the basis of rewards and punishments, the kind of persuasion which can masquer-
ade under the guise of personal choice, that is,
when the recipient is unaware that the situation or
environment has been fabricated or engineered to
produce specific forms of behaviour.

However, there appear to be three main weaknesses in Skinner's model of behaviour control or
modification for a theory of persuasion:
  (i) it leaves aside the factor of motivation
      and other cognitive variables which may
      have a bearing on behaviour;

(ii) it is not appropriate for dealing with
distance persuasion, e.g. press, radio,
television, because control over reinforcement, in terms of immediacy, is not
possible (distance persuasion is inevitably concentrated upon the stimulus side
of the stimulus-response formulation);

(iii) it concentrates upon closed systems, or
it requires tight control to be effective.

So far we have been concerned with two kinds of
learning models, conditioned and instrumental, both
of them are in the connectionist tradition, and both
of them can be interpreted as models for manipulat-
ing people. In Skinner's terms, the learner may
have the freedom to choose one form of response
rather than another, as long as he is prepared to
accept the consequences of his choice. A kind of
minimal freedom is available. Their relevance as
models for shaping behaviour is considerable for
closed or captive situations. In open, or so called
free societies, systematic control over the many
variables which affect human behaviour is not usually
feasible; in communication terms, the receiver has
options which he can exercise. For instance, he may
choose not to expose himself to a particular medium,
or the media themselves may present conflicting or
competing information. Therefore, the extreme manipulative elements possible in conditioned and instrumental learning are interesting to note, but in
normal non-coercive type situations where more freedom exists for individuals to set their own goals,
they are less to be feared. Skinner saw the whole
of human existence as being one in which contingencies and consequences bear down upon the individual,
but what we are particularly interested in is the
power of third parties to so arrange situations that
they can persuade others to behave in a pre-determined way or pattern.
    We have concentrated upon the stimulus-response
and reinforcement aspects of connectionist learning
theory but we shall now turn to a consideration of
not just the stimuli and the situational factors,
but to the thoughts or cognitions which mediate
between these. This moves us away from man as auto-
maton, to thinking man with hopes and expectations.

Intervening variables
The theory of conditioned and instrumental learning
provides no place for thought processes as the con-

nection between stimulus and response is discussed
only in terms of reinforcement. We know, however,
that the mental, internal state of any individual
plays an important part in determining the action
or response made in particular situations, or on
receipt of specific information. This is important
for a theory of persuasion as it draws attention to
intervening variables, the middle ground between
stimulus and response. The work of two influential
learning theorists, Hull (1952) and Tolman (1932,
1959), will be used here to illustrate this middle
ground.

Hull's work belongs to the connectionist tradition of learning theory, and as such it is closely
allied to the S-R tradition. However, it differs
in certain important respects from the Skinnerian
and Pavlovian models by the emphasis which Hull places upon intervening variables. Hull devised specific notations and mathematical formulae for defining learning behaviour. Here we shall direct our
attention to his principal concepts. According to
Hull, the likelihood of a particular response following a particular stimulus is conditioned upon
three factors: (i) the strength of the existing relationship, called habit strength, built up as a result of previous experience; (ii) the energy or vigour
with which performances are made, called drive; and
(iii) the size or magnitude of the expected reward,
called incentive motivation. These three variables
can produce what Hull termed a reaction potential.

Hull's work indicates that the likelihood of a
response being made to a particular persuasive appeal or situation is proportional to the combination
of existing habitual responses in the same situation,
to the internal drive state, and to expected reward.
These three variables provide the focus of many
advertisements, but their failure as targets for
appeals lies in the fact that the persuaders may
have no way of knowing the habit strengths, internal
drives, or the expected rewards which each individual
carries, and with which he faces appeals directed
towards him. Distance advertising can infer states,
and attempt to produce states, but it cannot know
them in fine detail, it must generalise.

In considering Tolman's work, we also switch
the emphasis of persuasion away from behaviourism in
its strictest sense towards concern with the cognitive state of the person, to his or her attitudes,
beliefs and goals. Tolman's (1932) most notable work
was written during the period when behaviourism was

in ascendancy, when one of the major concerns of learning theorists was precision of measurement in an attempt to make the study of human behaviour as near as possible to the methods of enquiry of the physical sciences. In such a milieu, Tolman retained an interest in the more speculative aspects of human behaviour, more speculative that is in terms of accuracy of measurement. In particular, it was to the concept of goals that Tolman directed his attention; this is of special interest here as advertising and propaganda frequently attempt to fix goals, or to modify them. Hill (1965, p.116) summarised Tolman's contribution as follows:

> Tolman's problem was to develop a theory for dealing with the complex variability of ... behaviour as it operates in search of goals. To do this, he considered it necessary to take account of the individual's cognitions, his perceptions and beliefs about the world... The existing behaviourist theory regarded anything intervening between the stimulus and response as itself a response just as physical and potentially just as measurable as any other response. If the word 'cognition' had any meaning at all for such behaviourists it was another name for the tiny movement of the speech muscles or else a figment of some sloppy mentalistic theorist's imagination. Tolman objected to both these meanings of cognition. He thought it should be possible to use the term cognition objectively without treating it as a physical, directly measurable movement. He therefore designated cognitions as intervening variables.

Tolman's emphasis on goals and expectancies is of significant concern to our theme of persuasion. The goals and expectancies that people carry with them bring us near to another major theme in this book, namely imagination; goals and expectancies are always future oriented, and in this way they relate to imagination, because it is only through imagination that the future can be apprehended. The work of Tolman is tied to the language of behaviourism, but it reaches out to include a more open or purposeful view of human behaviour.

According to Tolman learning falls into six categories:

      (i) the tendency to seek particular goals rather than others, owing to previous experience;

(ii) knowledge of the type of reinforcement, positive or negative that particular situations generate;

(iii) views about the structure of the 'world', what Tolman termed mental maps;

(iv) biases or preferments in the way or ways that people deal with situations;

(v) the ability to discriminate among drives; in other words being able to distinguish between various motives which propel action;

(vi) the learning of movement patterns, this refers to the formation of practical or manipulative skills.

From this list, there are a number of inferences for persuasion. In the first place, a knowledge of the previous experience of people can be used as the basis for setting goals. Secondly, attempts may be made to modify a person's expectations (this is the basis of many appeals, both commercial and political). Thirdly,persuasion can operate more effectively when it works through the preferred modes of learning of the recipients.

The expectations that people have about the structure of the world led Tolman to use the spatial metaphor 'mental maps' as an alternative to the technical term 'sign-gestalt'. Here we notice the influence of European theorising, the concept of gestalt being allied to American behaviourism. But, significantly, we see a withdrawal from the mechanistic model of learning, to one which is concerned with abstractions as represented by signs.

We shall pick up the significance of the sign in more detail in a later chapter when we come to deal with semiology, the study of signs and sign-systems. This will make a significant step forward for us, it will lead us to a theoretical understanding which is not reliant on psychology. We should, however, be aware of other directions which cognitive psychology has taken that are relevant to our theme. The work of Broadbent (1958) on selective learning, and Magoun (1969) on novelty is of particular significance. Broadbent put forward the notion of filtering of information as a complement to reinforcement. He suggested that the human perceptual system can be envisaged as having a 'filter' which selects particular stimuli at the expense of others. In terms of demands on the human perceptual system, it is not possible for all information to be accorded equal priority, therefore, some selection has to be made, and this is what Broadbent meant when he proposed a 'filter'. There are important implications here for our work, we can see that when faced with a range of stimuli the brain is compelled to select. But what will it select? It will select that which is deemed to be important, but it will also be alerted to novel events. The latter is a more transient phenomenon; novelty often gains our attention in the face of alternative presentations which are more predictable, but even so, the novel or the unexpected soon becomes the norm with repeated presentations, and thus loses its novel status. In terms of mediated information, we can observe the use of many techniques for gaining attention in the face of competing claims, banner headlines and unusual photographs are attempts to gain ascendancy in attention. This is not the whole picture as habits acquired over time can act as route finders, causing the individual to select in a pre-determined manner. This issue of selection pervades not only what people will attend to in the first place, but also what they remember. This is an issue that we will take up in more detail in the next chapter.

SUMMARY

1. Learning modifies the individual in some way or other, it creates change. To the extent that persuasion is directed towards changing the individual, whether it be in terms of beliefs, attitudes. or actions, then theories of learning are of relevance to the construction of a general theory of persuasion.

2. Learning is involved with the perception or conception of relationships. Persuasion is also concerned with creating relationships, this is observable in those advertisements which relate known and desirable characteristics to the product on offer.

3. Stimulus-Response learning theories are more relevant to persuasion which takes place in 'closed situations', that is, in situations where control over reinforcement can be systematic, without contamination from other non-controllable sources.

4. Beliefs, attitudes, goals and expectations need to be taken into consideration. They provide a special target for mediated information.

5. Individuals carry expectations and preferred modes of dealing with information.

6. The brain has a limited capacity for processing information, therefore, a selectivity bias arises which apportions priority to things of importance to the individual.

7. Novel presentations can gain initial impact in terms of attention, but with time, they become habituated and thus lose their novel status.

REFERENCES

BROADBENT, D.E. (1958) Perception and Communication. London: Pergamon.

HILL, W.F. (1965) Learning. London: Methuen.

HULL, C.L. (1952) A Behavior System. New York: Wiley.

MAGOUN, H.W. (1969) Advances in brain research with implications for learning. In Pribram, K.H. (ed.) On the Biology of Learning. New York: Harcourt, Brace & World, pp. 169-190.

PACKARD, V. (1978) The People Shapers. London: Futura.

SCHEIN, E.H., SCHNEIER, I. and BARKER, C.H. (1961) Coercive Persuasion. New York: W.W. Norton & Co.

SKINNER, B.F. (1938) The Behavior of Organisms. New York: MacMillan.

"   (1948) Walden Two. New York: MacMillan.

"   (1953) Science and Human Behavior. New York: MacMillan.

"   (1973) Beyond Freedom and Dignity. Harmondsworth: Penguin.

THORNDIKE, E.L. (1931) Human Learning. New York: Century.

TOLMAN, E.C. (1932) Purposive Behavior in Animals and Men. New York: Appleton-Century.

"   (1959) Principles of purposive behavior. In Koch, S. (ed.) Psychology: a study of a science. Vol. 2. General systematic formulations, learning and special processes. New York: McGraw-Hill, pp. 92-157.

Chapter Two

WHAT IS REMEMBERED?

Through the various forms of media in contemporary
society persuasive messages seek to command attention,
and to establish ideas or beliefs in the minds of
viewers or readers. When they are successful in
achieving these objectives, we may ask, how well is
the information or image remembered? For if it is
not remembered with sufficient intensity it will have
limited value as a persuasive force. The fallibility
of the human memory creates a problem for retaining
knowledge of all kinds, not merely that with persuasive intent. Therefore, an awareness of the nature
of human memory with its dual concepts of remembering and forgetting becomes an important factor in our
development of the theme of communication and persuasion. There are two possible approaches that we can
take, we can direct attention towards memory as a
psychological problem, or we can take a look at the
ways in which messages are constructed. It will be
seen from what follows that both approaches are intertwined. The form of a message or image can determine the degree of resistance to decay in memory,
and the existing mental state of any one individual
can also have a significant effect on what is remembered.
    We shall begin by focusing on the psychological
factors of memory. The term memory is often loosely
employed in a way which suggests a physical entity
with volumetric dimensions; or it is often referred
to as a property endowed through genetic inheritance.
It has also been portrayed (Pribram, 1969) as a two-
factor mechanism which deals separately with spatial
and temporal information, the whole being compared
with a physical artefact, the hologram. However,
in view of our interest in persuasion rather than
neurophysiology, it is the wider, non-mechanistic
aspects of memory that provides the focus for our

attention. We need to regard memory as a process
rather than an entity, because it is the process
itself which is open to modification, and thus to
persuasive influences. When the process is known,
or at least known with a little more clarity, we may
be in a position to determine with more precision
the effects that memory has upon its contents during
the passage of various lengths of time.

A useful introduction to work in the field of
memory is given by Hunter (1964); his overall view
was that memory is rather an ambiguous entity, but
that it contains one essential thread linking a past
experience to a present experience. It is about
'time'. But it is time understood in a personal way,
of relationships made between past and present experiences or activities. Why certain relationships are
recalled and not others is of special interest to our
theme.

Types of Memory

As a consequence of experimental research, memory
has been sub-divided into two category types, namely,
short-term and long-term. Short-term refers to those
events where information is retained for only a matter of seconds, for example, the mental registration
of a telephone number which we take on consulting a
telephone directory. Even within seconds the number
may have slipped from our memory, with the consequence that we need another glance at the printed number
in order to be able to recall it. In particular,
this is likely to happen when some form of interference intervenes between initial registration and the
act of dialling.

This short-term registration problem contrasts
with long-term retention, epitomized by the retention
which we possess in memory for those numbers used
repeatedly, or those of special importance to ourselves. Another common example of loss over the
short-term is that of advertisements which are beyond
recall even when seen on a television screen only a
short time before. This problem of short-term retention is related directly to what is known as the
'span of immediate memory', the neurological limits
set on our capacity for processing information.
Miller (1967), using concepts and measures provided
by information theory, came to the conclusion that
the span of immediate memory and the span of absolute
perceptual judgement impose severe limitations on the
amount of information that we are able to receive,
process and remember. Nevertheless, although these
limits exist, it is possible by a process known as

'chunking', that is, grouping items together into some system, pattern or organisation, to extend the amount of information that can be handled, and subsequently recalled. In other words, the systematic ordering of information by setting-up relationships reduces randomness.

In addition to the 'chunking' or ordering technique just mentioned, other factors may influence memory both in the short term and the long term. For example, the expectation which is made regarding the likelihood of re-use of information is an important factor in retention; as we should expect, the greater the expectation of re-use, the more likely it becomes that information will be committed to more than short-term memorisation. There are negative effects, such as fatigue, distraction, and unfamiliarity with the material to be remembered, which have inhibiting effects on memory. What is clear, however, is that neurological limits set a ceiling on the amount of information that can be processed and retained, and that human memory is susceptible to disruption from other peripheral activities which compete for the limited processing resources of the brain.

Once the barrier of short-term retention is passed, that is, when information is stored in some relatively permanent way which is less subject to competing demands in storage, we can speak of long-term retention having been effected. However, even then, long-term retention poses particular problems of its own which we shall be dealing with later. From the standpoint of persuasion, it is apparent that messages should be able to surmount the particular restrictions of short-term retention; for example, information that makes too high a demand upon discrimination, going beyond the span of immediate memory, and with little or no 'chunking' supplied, is likely to be only partially received, if at all. Likewise, distractions, technically known as 'noise' in communication theory, are likely to have similar disruptive effects. Long-term retention is subject to competition from new information, but of overriding significance is the desire or motivation to retain information, and as we shall see in a later chapter, motivation itself has sinews stemming in many directions.

Three phases of memory

Remembering, as a process, can be divided into three distinct phases: (i) reception (learning); (ii) retention (storing); and (iii) retrieval (which may be through recall or recognition), or as it is sometimes

called reproduction. It will be seen, therefore,
that the last stage, the actual representation to
consciousness of stored information cannot be effective if the earlier stages have not established the
proper conditions.
     Even at the reception or learning phase, prev-
ious learning experiences play a part in determining
how information is registered. Of crucial importance
is the initial disposition to attend, or, in Pribram's
(1964) terms the state of 'readiness'. This takes
place against potentially meaningful ideas and information which already exists in memory. This can
lead to difficulties at the outset, particularly when
the new information cannot find reference points for
attachment. In consequence,erroneous meanings may
emerge because of the unavailability of relevant
connections or anchoring points. Information becomes meaningless when it cannot find at least some
connection with what is already established in the
mind of the recipient. It follows, therefore, that
effective persuasion has the task of establishing
the mental maps or cognitive frameworks of its audience in order for connections to be established,or,
to use a nautical metaphor, for anchoring to be achieved. The essential point is that persuasive communications, and indeed all effective communications,
need to be structured in such a way that they make
connections with established concepts in the minds
of the receivers. The more the connections, the
more immediate is comprehension likely to be.
     Turning to the second phase of remembering, that
of retention, we can note that newly learned information is assimilated more firmly into the existing
cognitive structure, but its likelihood of being
retained is proportional to the degree of anchorage
which it can find; the more extensive or the richer
the associations the greater is the potential. On
the other hand, there is a tendency towards attenuation of newly assimilated information, that is, it
tends to become less qualified and more similar to
the anchoring ideas to which it becomes attached. At
this stage, information goes into a state of latency,
available for recall or re-use, but only under certain conditions. The retention of information can
be guided by a number of considerations. For example,
what is felt to be important can gain priority in the
limited capacity of the store, this is a personal
decision, although others may suggest importance for
their own motives, e.g. advertisers. Other factors
aiding retention are repetition and vividness in presentation.

20

What is Remembered?

From reception and retention, we now turn to a
consideration of the third and final phase, namely
retrieval. Retrieval stands upon the shoulders, so
to speak, of the two earlier or preceding phases of
memory as one cannot recall what one has not learned
or retained. Factors contributing to what is actually recalled are, on the one hand, the perceived
requirements of the present situation, and, on the
other hand, physiological states such as tiredness
(Hunter, 1964). Two unique category differences
operate at the retrieval phase, namely, recall and
recognition. Both need separate consideration, and
we shall find that the difference has an important
implication for our study of persuasion, particularly
the use of memory aids or prompts at points of sale,
and in conditions of a social kind, reminders like
those about safety factors in close proximity to
points of danger.

Recall is remembering without any perceptual
assistance, for example, the ability to remember the
appearance of a person in their absence, to remember
by drawing upon mental memories, a condition such as
one experiences when thinking or imagining with closed eyes. Recall does not require any physical stimuli, at least not external stimuli; it is contained
within the mental life of the individual, but of
course, it can be prompted into action as the result
of external circumstances, as when one is asked to
recall an event because of some current happening.
Recall is always a task of reconstruction, and because this is so it opens avenues for imaginative or
idiosyncratic interpretations. It can, for example,
re-arrange the seriality of experience, by placing
events out of their original sequence, inverting the
order of things. It can also collapse separate events into one episode; thus it may appear to be able
to override history, or at least give it a particular order, one which satisfies the motivation of the
individual. It is a fallible process, being based
in the first place on a learning process which itself
is error prone, and in the second place on a retention
system which possesses the potential to distort info-
mation.

Recognition is remembering with perceptual assistance, which is the opposite to the condition of
recall. It involves identifying through a present
sensory experience and is less taxing than recall
because, unlike recall, restrictions are placed on
the references for search in memory. A framework
for interpretation is already presented, thus, in
terms of information theory, there are fewer choices

to be made with a resultant easing of the load in mental processing. Whereas recall requires a mental search of a wide range of stored information, recognition can borrow a range of media or artefacts to help as memory prompts, for example, verbal notices, symbolic images, or a combination of the two.

Symbols as recognition aids can reduce information into a more compact form, and thus speed up the process of comprehension. Compare, for instance, the time taken to read a verbally coded traffic notice with a symbolic representation conveying the same information. Symbols are not read sequentially, and they carry information in such a way that they can trigger-off concepts with a limited number of clues, that is, when the receiver is familiar with their structure and their intended meaning. Symbols possess the potential to organise thoughts, when they fail to do this they appear as artefacts, but not as symbols. Organising or ordering has implications for learning and remembering, as Miller (1967, p.19) wrote, 'it is helpful to organize material intelligently before we memorise it; the process of organization enables us to package the same total amount of information into fewer symbols, and so ease the task of remembering'.

Recognition, like all the forms that memory takes, is selective as through past experience and through personal motivation the individual creates biases which orientate him to recognize more intently certain things, people or places, rather than others. This tendency to bias is a natural corollary to life, it would be a very strange person who gave equal weighting to everything encountered. Bias can also be given by third parties and this is particularly obvious in political propaganda. Bias can be considered as a 'funnelling of attention' and it was seen by Hunter (1964, p.35) to play a part in social conditioning. He wrote:

the more narrowly prepared a person is to recognise one kind of event, the more rapidly and correctly will he recognize this kind of event when it occurs; and the more slowly and incorrectly will he recognize an event of another kind... what we recognize in any person's actions, say selfishness or selflessness, is influenced by what we are prepared to recognize in him. The aim of social propaganda, like that of the stage magician, is to prepare people to recognize events in some ways and not others.

Of course, preparing people to see things in particular ways rather than others should not only be seen in terms of social propaganda with its sinister overtones of manipulation. Much of educational experience is given to directing attention to particular points of view, and thus it could be said to be biasing people into prescribed modes.

Bias or selective attention is a normal process in our lives, with the word bias carrying a more emotive 'ring' than selective attention, but be that as it may, whichever term we select, the tendency still exists. In fact, in Broadbent's (1958) theorising on the nature of perception and communication, the process of selective attention is central to his theme, he likened the process to a filter, suggesting that perceptual information is given some kind of priority by which certain information is 'filtered' and allowed to proceed for further processing at the expense or to the exclusion of other information.

Individual biases

To be effective, persuasion has to overcome the various forms of resistance set-up by memory, in particular it has to contend with the various stages of memorisation which we have discussed; it has to be received, retained, and be available for recall or for use in recognition. Moreover, even when these phases are recognised, there still exist the personal or idiosyncratic ways in which people integrate new ideas or information within their particular cognitive framework; bias can operate at each of the three levels. Bias operates even at the outset, with the tendency for individuals to impose their own meaning in accordance with the requirements of the situation.

Search for meaning

From his work on memory, Bartlett (1932) maintained that there exists a tendency for people to attach meaning to events even when such events are ambiguous, as though ambiguity is a thing to be avoided at all costs. The meaning given is of course aided by the frames of reference (called 'schemata' by Bartlett) of the individual. The avoidance of ambiguity could be considered a way of easing decision making or perceptual load, which, to many, is a more desirable state than one of incomprehension or confusion. Bartlett saw two influences working upon memory, cultural and personal, both presenting frameworks for interpretation, these are:

      (i) that memory is influenced by idiosyncratic
          and culturally biased schemata;

and
(ii) there is a tendency for recall to demonstrate imaginative reconstructions
which are meaningful to the individual
concerned.

The search for meaning in terms appropriate to the
receiver and in terms not envisaged by the sender
calls attention to the possibilities of modification
that messages may undergo 'in transit', thus producing discrepancy between what the message originator
intended, and what the receiver actually interpreted.
We shall be looking at meaning as a concept
later, but we should note here that meaning is bound
up with the cognitive structure as it exists in the
individual. It is from this existence, and not from
some ideal state that connections are made in the
establishment of extended meaning. The existing cognitive structure provides anchorage for new ideas or
information, an anchorage which can serve to mitigate
decay in stored memories. The making of connections
or the search for anchorage within the individual's
mental framework is a task facing educationists and
others with less disinterested intentions. In particular, we can notice from the work of Ellul (1973)
on propaganda how the propagandist sets out to reach
his audience in terms familiar to themselves, and
thus find an anchorage in a 'receptive harbour'.
Thus two objectives are achieved, first of all meaning is established in, or through, the way the propagandist's audience sees the world, and secondly,
the message is more likely to be remembered because
of its attachment to an existing pattern of thought.

Ordering effects

Thus far, we have focused our attention on some of
the main psychological aspects of memory. Now we
will turn our attention to the effects of message
construction as a factor in remembering. One significant area of study related to persuasion is that
of the order in which information is presented. For
example, what do people remember most, things they
hear at the beginning of a lecture/talk/sermon/tele-
vision programme, or things they hear at the end?
Hunter (1964) found that items at the beginning
of a list are remembered quicker than those at the
end, but those at the end tend to be remembered with
less effort than those in the middle. However, certain other factors can intervene to produce contrary
effects, for example, the degree of 'strikingness'
of particular items or parts. This particular tendency could be explained by invoking the factor of

novelty which both Broadbent (1968) and Magoun (1969)
mentioned as a factor in human attention, that is,
the tendency to process novel stimuli at the expense
of the familiar. Of course, unless the initially
novel stimulus is changed it will very soon lose its
novel status, and thus become one of the others. The
main implication from the studies of serial-position
effects is that items which are of most importance
should, preferably, be placed early on, unless 'stri-
king' effects are included which can override the
positional effects.

The next point we need to consider relates to
messages which contain, within the message, arguments
for and against a particular position or point of
view, commonly known as pro-con arguments. Work in
this area was first carried out by Lund as early as
1925. He presented subjects with messages containing
pro and con arguments on various issues. For experimental purposes, he presented fifty-percent of the
messages in the order pro followed by con, and the
other fifty-percent were given in the reverse order,
i.e. con followed by pro. As a result of these experiments, Lund found that the side presented first,
irrespective of whether it was in the form of pro or
con, was the most influential, or, from our perspective, the most persuasive. Lund's finding was refin-
ed in later years, for example when Hovland (1957)
reported the combined findings from different studies
which showed that the side of an issue presented
first is likely to have a disproportionate influence
on opinion under the following conditions:

    (i) when clues as to the incompatibility of
        different items of information are absent;

  (ii) when the contradictory information is
        presented by the same communicator;

 (iii) when committing actions are taken after
        only one side of the issue has been pre-
        sented;

  (iv) when the issue is an unfamiliar one;

   (v) when the recipient has only a superficial
        interest in the issue.

In terms of propagandist effects, the studies
reported by Hovland suggest that where the controversial nature of the issue is not mentioned, or where
exposure to other points of view is minimized, either
through self-selection by the individuals concerned,
or through monopoly control of information, primacy
effects are likely to be produced. The variety

of influences at work in propaganda are dealt with
more fully in a later chapter, but it is worth not-
ing here that persuasive influences may operate in
a variety of ways; for instance, a part of a message
could be made more interesting than another, or a
part could be made with more vigour, and, thereby,
be perceived more strongly. This is the kind of condition with which advocates in the courts of law are
familiar; it is also a condition familiar to the pol-
itician in his adversarial role.

Inhibition
Studies in the area of memory have highlighted the
place of inhibition as an important factor in the
ability to recall information. Inhibition can work
retroactively, that is the effect caused by present
or current learning on what has been learnt earlier,
or it may work in the opposite direction, that is,
with earlier learning having an effect upon the recall of currently learnt information, this condition
of inhibition is known as proactive. According to
Pribram (1964) consolidation of information in memory
is a two-fold process. The first or initial phase
takes place mainly during the first hour, during which
time the information to be remembered is still 'frag-
ile'. And at this time, consolidation of the new
information may be subject to either retroactive or
proactive inhibition. At one time it was generally
assumed that retroactive rather than proactive inhibition was the most disruptive influence on memor-
ization. However, Underwood (1964) suggested the
opposite. His argument was that acquired habits
interfere with present events. Of course, acquired
habits are not always at variance with present needs,
they can be highly relevant as props to learning and
remembering. Therefore, one needs to be careful not
to generalise too broadly in the interpretation of
these arguments relating to the place of retroactive
and proactive inhibition.

Assimilation
Incoming messages are assimilated into an existing
framework of ideas or cognitions, they are not free
to have a life of their own. Furthermore, as we saw
earlier, there exists a bias which, through personal
experience, can cause preferential ways of dealing
with information, and this can be habit forming.
Habits conserve energy by reducing the demands upon
the individual's thought processes, and upon physical
energy in certain manual activities. In the same way,
we can see how, by a process of assimilation into an

existing structure, a similar economy of effort is achieved in memory. It is a reductionist tendency, and it was seen as such by Ausubel (1968, p.93) when he wrote:

> ...it is more economical and less burdensome merely to retain the more stable and established anchoring concepts and propositions than to remember the new ideas that are assimilated to them, the meaning of the new ideas tends to be assimilated or reduced, over the course of time, to the more stable meanings of the established anchoring ideas.

We have dealt with some, but by no means all of the factors relating to memory; it is an extensive field and one has to be selective in choosing those fields or areas of study which appear to have implications for our general theme of persuasion. Let us pick out some of the critical factors which have emerged here. First of all, for things or ideas to be remembered assurance has to be obtained that learning has actually taken place; secondly, there has to be some assurance that what is to be learned can find some connection or anchorage within the existing cognitive structures of the audience/receivers, otherwise retention will be inhibited, and learning difficult.

Of course, there are many techniques for aiding memory, for example by repetition of a message, by creating associations with other ideas, by the use of conventional symbols, and by making connections between the different senses (synaesthesia). An example of this is the visual advertisement which asks the viewer to feel the smoothness of the product on offer, at which point a hand will be shown caressing it; this is only a visual experience in terms of television viewing, but it can translate itself through synaesthesia into a 'felt' experience. Commercial persuaders frequently turn to these techniques, witness the repeated advertisements, the use of imagery and symbols, and evocation calling upon sensory memories of things and experiences in the past.

However, despite all the various ideas and thoughts about the nature of memory, there is one critical factor that is central to the whole issue, and that is motivation. Without motivation, or when it is minimal, the need to create a strong memory of things is diminished. It affects all aspects of persuasion, not only memory. In the next chapter we shall turn to a more careful scrutiny of some of the bases of motivation.

SUMMARY

1. Memory can be divided into three phases: (i) reception; (ii) retention; (iii) retrieval, which can be effected through either recall or recognition.

2. New information is connected or anchored to an existing cognitive structure. The richer the associations, the greater the likelihood of retention.

3. Recognition is less demanding than recall because it involves a more restricted mental search.

4. Individuals possess a bias in attending to, and retaining information. This is known as selective attention and selective retention.

5. Information remembered may be subject to idiosyncratic and imaginative reconstructions.

6. The order in which information is received can have an effect upon its retention. 'Strikingness' can also play a part in the retention of particular items.

REFERENCES

AUSUBEL, D.P. (1968) Educational Psychology. New York: Holt, Rinehart & Winston.

BARTLETT, F.C. (1932) Remembering. Cambridge: University of Cambridge Press.

BROADBENT, D.E. (1958) Perception and Communication. London: Pergamon Press.

ELLUL, J. (1973) Propaganda. New York: Vintage Books.

HOVLAND, C.I. (1957) Order of Presentation in Persuasion. New Haven: University of Yale Press.

HUNTER, I.M.L. (1964) Memory. Harmondsworth: Penguin Books.

LUND, F.H. (1925) The psychology of belief: a study of its emotional and volitional determinants. Journal of Abnormal and Social Psychology, vol. 20, pp. 174-196.

MAGOUN, H.W. (1969) Advances in brain research with implications for learning. In Pribram, K.H.(ed.) On the Biology of Learning. New York: Harcourt, Brace & World, pp. 169-190.

MILLER, G.A. (1967) The Psychology of Communication. Harmondsworth: Penguin Books.

PRIBRAM, K.H. (1964) Neurological notes on the art of educating. In Hilgard, E.R. (ed.) Theories of Learning and Instruction. Chicago: University of Chicago Press, pp. 78-110.

What is Remembered?

PRIBRAM, K.H. (1969) The four R's of remembering.
    In Pribram, K.H. (ed.) On the Biology of Learn-
    ing. New York: Harcourt, Brace & World,
    pp. 191-225.
UNDERWOOD, B.J. (1964) Laboratory studies in verbal
    learning. In Hilgard, E.R. (ed.) Theories of
    Learning and Instruction. Chicago: University
    of Chicago Press, pp. 133-152.

Chapter Three

THE IMPORTANCE OF MOTIVATION

Learning and retention of meaningful information is
strongly affected by motivation; motivation provides
the energy, psychologically speaking, for the efficiency of both processes; minimal motivation tends to
inhibit both learning and retention. The effectiveness of persuasion is also dependent upon the extent
to which it can enlist motivational support; even
under the extreme conditions of coercive persuasion,
motivation to avoid punishment is a classical means
of behavioural shaping. However, persuasion is generally directed towards positivity and it is enhanc-
ed to the extent that it can create or arouse positive motivation, motivation to attend, motivation to
learn, and motivation to remember. Various theories
have been put forward to explain the phenomenon of
motivation, and various techniques are exploited in
an attempt to make communications persuasive. Here
we shall trace the various approaches which have
been made in the study of motivation, and we shall
attempt to bring out their significances for a general theory of persuasion.
    Motivation has, metaphorically speaking, exten-
sive sinews in the fabric of human thought and behaviour; it has bases in both man's innate and learned
behaviour; it operates, or so it appears, at both
conscious and unconscious levels. The diverse origins of motivation are reflected in the variety of
ways in which persuasive appeals are constructed.
Such appeals may be directed to primitive, innate
needs, or to learned needs, technically known as
secondary needs. They may be overt, directed at
conscious aspirations, or covert, directed at deep-
seated unconscious desires. Theories of motivation
have tended to encompass this wide canvas, with experimental studies stressing the associative or learned component and clinical studies tending to emphasize

the more deep-seated levels of consciousness. However, there does appear to be one concept which is common to all theories of motivation, and that is the concept of motivation as the energiser of behaviour. As a process it can be likened to energy used in the propulsion of vehicles, it gives power to that which is otherwise inert. This is a rather simplified illustration, and as we shall see, motivational energy of a human kind cannot be specified in quantities, but can only be inferred as a result of human behaviour.

Need

A concept basic to the study of motivation is that of need. Need, or in its less extreme form, 'desire', produces instability in the relationship between a person and the environment. It is this instability which is presumed to have motivational properties, that is, properties which can be brought into play to reduce need or needs, and thereby restore stability or equilibrium. For instance, the need for food produces a state whereby the individual is motivated to seek satisfaction by the consumption of food, and hence restore a state of balance as regards food requirements. This can be conceived in cybernetic or homeostatic terms as the condition of equilibrium, the return to balance after discrepancy in a system, in this instance the human system. We are all familiar with the variety of innate conditions such as hunger, thirst and tiredness, which create the need for food, liquid and sleep. But the human condition is not merely one of acquiescence with the resolution of such states, it is one which, in normal conditions, may set out to arouse or create disequilibrium or instability in its relationship with the environment, and thereby consciously induce a personally generated state of imbalance. Here we refer to curiosity and ludic behaviour (Berlyne, 1960) which are desired for their own sake; and because they manifest themselves throughout the variety of human social conditions, we can speculate that they, like physiological demands, are also innate.

Innate needs, being genetically determined, arise spontaneously; but through a process of learning individuals acquire secondary needs. The creation of secondary needs is a prime objective of commercial persuaders. In developed societies, innate needs generally find fulfilment for the majority of the populace, but secondary or acquired needs, because they can be generated through the process of learning, allow scope for the employment of media

as interventionist devices directed towards the
creation of arbitrary needs.

Drive

The terms need and drive as used in motivational analysis are closely related, need being used to refer
to an unstable equilibrium in the relationship between an individual and the environment, such a need
being either innate or acquired. Drive, on the other
hand, is a theoretical conception which refers to the
activity engendered by need (Hebb, 1958); it refers
to the energy expended in the satisfaction of need.
Needs then are pre-requisites for drives, but it is
drives which are thrown into action when a need arises. Motivation refers to the general state or
process which determines the allocation of energy
to particular responses rather than others. The
determination of such responses is subject to learning and to the related concept of reinforcement, i.e.
the allocation of energy to produce a response is,
at least partially, dependent on the likelihood of
reinforcement. According to Miller and Dollard (1964,
p. 52), 'Drive impels the person to make responses...
whether these responses will be repeated depends on
whether or not they are rewarded. If the response
is not rewarded, the tendency to repeat it is weak-
ened.' The same process can be observed in the negative instance of drive to avoid punishment, if the
drive produces action which brings about a cessation
or lessening of punishment, then such action is likely to be employed on future and similar occasions.
However, if such action does not produce a desired
outcome, that is, it goes unrewarded, then it is
likely to become weaker on subsequent occasions.

The subjective probabilities which individuals
carry, in the light of their experience, can be seen
to produce a motivational weighting. In fact, Feather
(1965, p.201) included subjective probability as one
of three multiplicative factors in a generalised
equation of motivation, the other two being motive
(reason) and incentive (value). In the light of
Feather's threefold characteristics of motivation,
communications of a persuasive kind could be weighted
on one or a combination of these variables. It
would follow that the most persuasive, that is the
one possessing greatest motivational potency, would
be the one in which motive is strong, the expectation or probability of achieving a particular effect
is high, and one in which the outcome itself is
highly desirable. Feather's postulate is speculative, but it does provide a wider basis for the

assessment of persuasive communications than a mere
one-dimensional appraisal. For instance, the assessment of advertisements merely on their arousal potential, without taking into account probabilities and
incentive value, is likely to miss important variables in their evaluation. Of course, advertisements
can be directed to imagination, and hence create
illusory expectations and incentive values inflated
by the employment of imagery which may prompt action,
but such imagery would have to withstand the decay
in memory induced by the lapse of time; illusions
induced by media of all kinds can have a very short
life (tears are not long to dry on leaving the cinema).

The general power or motivational potency of
persuasive communications appears to reside in the
awareness that individuals do not merely desire to
satisfy needs and produce a steady-state according
to the homeostatic model, but that individuals seek
stimulation, as Getzels (1964, p.254) wrote, '[an
individual] is clearly often intrigued and challenged
by what is new and will go out of his way to encounter, explore, and master that which is intriguing
and challenging'.

The two apparently conflicting views that (a)
motivation is the energy available to produce homeostasis, and (b) that it is the availability of energy for exploration and/or stimulation, can be reconciled on the basis that normal individuals possess
both propensities which may materialise at different
times and/or in different circumstances. Therefore,
it is reasonable to expect that communications with
a persuasive intention can direct themselves to either of these states - one directed towards the satisfaction derived from quiescence, the other towards
the type of satisfaction which stems from stimulation.

Evidence for the effectiveness of appeals to
drives does not always reveal a linear correlation
between the strength of the appeal and the behavioural outcome. For example, the work of Hovland et al
(1953) on appeals to fear shows that it can be coun-
ter-productive when it is pressed too far. They
wrote (p.83), 'Experiments indicate that when the
goal of persuasive communication is to create sustained preferences or attitudes, a relatively low degree
of fear arousal will sometimes be the optimal level,
that too strong a fear appeal can evoke some form of
interference which reduces the effectiveness of the
communication.'

Dissonance

Included in the homeostatic tradition of theorising

33

on motivation is the theory of cognitive balance. Theories in this tradition are based on the assumption that individuals tend to strive for equilibrium, although not necessarily consciously. This drive towards balance is regarded by cognitive theorists as a source of motivational energy; therefore it can be conceived as having drive potential. Many persuasive appeals, particularly of the commercial type, can be seen to be addressing themselves to this balance tendency. For example, advertisements which suggest dissatisfaction with present material conditions attempt to raise conflicting cognitions within the individual and, thereby, to produce discrepancies between existing attitudes.

In the psychological literature (Cohen, 1964) three theoretical models are put forward to account for cognitive balance, their technical labels being: (i) principle of congruity; (ii) balance model; and (iii) cognitive dissonance. Of particular importance to our interest in persuasion is cognitive dissonance, because it focuses upon the internal cognitions of individuals, the conditions which arouse dissonance, and the ways in which dissonance can be reduced.

The theory of cognitive dissonance was first formulated by Festinger (1957) who sees dissonance as arising in at least three separate ways: (i) logical inconsistency; (ii) inconsistency between an attitude and a behaviour; and (iii) the disconfirmation of an expectation. This latter is of interest to commercial persuaders whose appeals may produce unwanted dissonance, that is, when expectations raised by publicity are not fulfilled, thus reducing future motivational potency because of lowered expectation of achievement, as specified in Feather's motivational model.

While Festinger suggested three ways by which dissonance can be raised, there are at least three ways by which it can be reduced: (i) the rationalisation of a situation; (ii) the search for additional information which is consonant or supportive of existing behaviour; and (iii) elimination or altering of dissonant elements. The latter can be achieved by forgetting or suppressing the dissonant element, or alternatively, by the altering of existing attitudes, opinions or beliefs.

While dissonance theory is interesting and important in terms of the kind of motivation which can be arbitrarily raised by a third party for the purpose of attempting the revision of cognitions, for example, an attempted switch in 'brand' loyalties through an advertisement, it is, as a theory, not without its critics. For instance, McGinnies (1974) suggested that it raises the question whether we are trained to be consistent from childhood by means of rewards and punishments, thus implying a social dimension. Berlyne (1960, pp. 284 & 285) suggested that it seems better to invoke the more general notion of conflict than that of dissonance. He went on to propose that cognitive imbalance can be reduced by reorganising attitudes and beliefs in the following ways:

Denial. The evaluation of one of the elements involved is changed. For example, a man who would like both to be slim and to eat rich food but realises that it is impossible to satisfy both likes, professes that he never liked rich foods anyway.

Bolstering. One of the elements is linked with other ideas that are associated with strong attitudes and with whose assistance the opposing belief or evaluation can be outweighed. For example, the smoker who is worried about lung cancer decides that smoking is a bad habit and costs too much money.

Differentiation. A distinction is made within one of the conflicting elements, such that some aspect of it is valued positively and the other negatively. For example, a tendency to believe in the truth of the Bible and a tendency to believe in the theory of evolution are reconciled by differentiating literal truth and figurative truth, and attributing only the latter to the Bible.

Transcendence. Conflicting elements are combined into some larger unit which is collectively viewed with favour or disfavour. For example, a partiality for both science and religion, perceived as leading in opposite directions, may give rise to the feeling that a well-rounded life requires the cultivation of both.

Berlyne suggested that the concept of dissonance can be included in the more general notion of conflict which itself can find one form of relief by the acquisition of knowledge. He further suggested that the various theories of cognitive balance, including dissonance, are alike in recognizing that beliefs, attitudes, and other symbolic processes of an individual do not exist in isolation but interact, and that there can be discrepancies between them that the individual is motivated to remedy. From this it

follows that persuasive communications can be addressed to beliefs, that is, knowledge based on
reasoning, or to emotive evaluations. The dissonance, or in Berlyne's terms, the conflict engendered
when beliefs are brought into question, can be used
to serve motivational purposes, in this case motivation to reduce the cognitive conflict.

The arousal of dissonance and the proffering of
resolutions, overt or covert, is one of the aims of
advertising and propaganda. However, as mentioned
earlier, individuals may naturally seek stimulation
and eschew the satisfaction of equilibrium; on this
basis, persuasive appeals would be directed to curiosity, including the possibility of risk-taking.
Dissonance theory is essentially in the homeostatic
tradition, whereas arousal theory (Berlyne, 1960)
is based on man's need for stimulation. However,
we need not seek a resolution to these opposing
theoretical positions if we posit behaviour as a
linear process in which departures are made from,
and returns made towards, a steady state. In other
words, balance or consistency would follow upon a
period of arousal, and vice versa. In these terms,
effective persuasion would not seek constantly to
stimulate, but would allow for periods of return to
quiescence, that is, to a steady state.

A hierarchy of needs

We have seen that drive reduction is not an adequate
way in which to explain the totality of man's motivational make-up, we are forced to consider those
aspects of man's motivational bases which act to
spur him on, even in the face of apparently satisfied
material conditions. A parallel can be made, for
example, with the well-fed and well-housed cat which
prefers to leave the cosiness of its shelter for the
excitement of the night's prowl, despite the weather
conditions and other unknown eventualities. The need
in this case is not satisfied by one episode, it is
a continuous need for exploration, it is dynamic,and
while it may undergo temporary satisfaction, it will
persist in repeating itself. There is no end state;
the activity itself is the goal.

The work of Maslow (1962) has implications for
theorising on persuasion, although it appears rather
speculative as it is based mostly upon clinical res-
earches and personal experience rather than upon formal experimentation. Maslow's work is essentially
developmental, whereas Berlyne's work is more in the
neuropsychological tradition of Hebb (1949),who emphasised the place of sensory stimulation in normal

healthy living.

Maslow (1955) maintained that motivation can be placed on a hierarchical basis of needs, the lowest in the hierarchy being physiological needs, rising progressively to psychological needs of a personal kind which he termed self-actualisation. His theorising arose as a response to the then current emphasis upon behaviourism. He wrote (p.14):

> What is lacking here (by here, he meant drive-reduction theory or, as he termed it, 'deficiency-need gratification') is awareness of the dynamic principle which ties together and interrelates all these separate motivational episodes. The different basic needs are related to each other in a hierarchical order such that gratification of one need and its consequent removal from the centre of the stage brings about not a state of rest or stoic apathy, but rather the emergence into consciousness of another 'higher' need; wanting and desiring continues but at a higher level.

In Maslow's terms, deficiency-need gratification tends to be episodic and climactic, whereas motivation can be considered to operate at a number of progressive levels, with one following upon another in an interrelated or dynamic way; this he termed 'growth-motivation'. In terms of the consumer oriented society, persuasive appeals with their climactic promises could be said to belong to deficiency-need gratification. Deficiency-needs can be artificially created by advertising, and their satisfaction arranged through the provision of goods or services. However, when commercially induced needs are created, the motivational energy or drive which will be made available for the individual to take the necessary action to satisfy the need will still depend on the other factors given in Feather's (1965) equation, that is, (a) the subjective probability of achieving the outcome, and (b) the incentive value as perceived by the individual.

Maslow's thesis on motivation centres around two main concepts: (i) needs are developmental; and (2) they are hierarchical. However, the hierarchy to which he refers is not one through which the individual advances step by step, but should be considered more like an elevator which can ascend or descend to appropriate levels according to the demands of the moment. There is, according to Maslow, a preferential basis in their unfolding, with the

highest need for self-actualisation resting upon the
continual gratification of primary needs, which are
always there even if only in a state of latency.
From this it follows that regression to lower needs
always remains a possibility, and this is necessary
for the well being of the 'whole person'. From this
it follows that motivation at the higher levels is
only likely to be induced in individuals who have
obtained satisfaction of their more basic needs, for
example, safety and security, and that appeals directed towards the more basic needs stand a greater
chance of being responded to when it is known that
such needs have not been satisfied. It would, however, be unusual to find appeals directed towards
basic needs in western societies, except in the case
of charity appeals for third world countries. Appeals to the need for safety, however, can be seen in
advertisements stressing the security of home-owner-
ship. At the less basic level, appeals through advertisements can be found stressing love and affec-
tion; and at the higher, so-called self-actualising
or growth-motivated level, appeals can be found
stressing individual self-fulfilment as a state in
its own right, although even here, when there is a
commercial element, one may begin to suspect an appeal to deficiency motivation. In general, the meta-
motivation implied by Maslow's self-actualisation
theory appears to belong more to the realm of per-
sonalised idealism. It is a rare individual who has
no dependency on others, and such dependency brings
in its train the beginnings of deficiency-motivation
and hence the cyclical process of homeostasis.

For a theory of persuasion, Maslow's concepts
point to the unfolding of higher needs as those lower
in the 'need hierarchy' are gratified. It should be
stressed that Maslow sees descent to lower needs not
as pathological but a natural process of healthy
living. Thus guilt feelings over regression to more
primitive needs can be dissipated. According to Maslow, man's higher nature rests upon man's lower nature,
needing it as a foundation. The best way to develop
this higher nature is to fulfil and gratify the lower
nature first. The implication here is that man's
nature, ideals, aspirations and abilities rest not
upon instinctual renunciation, but rather upon its
gratification. Here we can see some identity of thought between the work of Maslow and that of Freud,
and it is to the work of Freud that we shall now turn
for further insights into motivational analysis, for
the purpose of developing further our analysis of
persuasive communications.

The Importance of Motivation

Unconscious processes

In recent years, reviews of techniques of persuasion
(Packard, 1962, 1978) have stressed the importance
of motivation stemming from unconscious origins.
Freud postulated that all behaviour is motivated and
goal-directed, and he laid particular emphasis upon
degrees of consciousness which he illustrated through
the use of a spatial metaphor, the three levels being:
(i) perceptual consciousness, present awareness through the senses; (ii) preconsciousness, that which,
although presently not available to consciousness,
is capable of recall when required; (iii) unconsciou-
sness, that which cannot be brought into awareness
because it is actively repressed. Through the analysis of dreams and other indirect avenues of intro-
spection, Freud concluded that motivation has its
mainsprings in the unconscious. And for our interest
in persuasion, we can take note of the comment made
by Eriksen (1958, p.169) when he wrote, '...note the
current interest and activity among hucksters of
Madison Avenue over the possibility of being able
to manipulate the buying habits of a large segment
of the population through advertising that appeals
to or is directed at the subliminal or unconscious
level.'   •
     The deliberate attempt to carry out persuasion
at the deeper levels of consciousness can be considered, psychologically speaking, as a form of hidden
persuasion; that is, persuasion which appeals to the
less rational side of human consciousness, to the
preconscious and unconscious levels. Freud also
placed special emphasis on the importance of deep-
seated memories, and the symbolic representation of
suppressed thoughts which may be made manifest in
dreams. He also placed particular stress on associations and imagery. Such ideas are germane to the
persuader; ideas of association, symbolism and pictorial imagery can be utilized in appeals to the preconscious and unconscious. It is assumed by professional persuaders that the motivational energy contained at these levels can be tapped for purposes of
their own design.
     However, evidence of the effect of such appeals
is hard to obtain; there are so many contaminating
variables contributing to the responses that people
make to persuasive communications. But a review of
commercial advertising, particularly of cosmetics,
provides plenty of evidence of the attempt to utilise
deep-seated motivations. The dream-like quality of
much of popular advertising can be accounted for in
Freudian terms; the gaining of access to the uncons-

cious through symbolism and irrational possibilities
can be given credence when analysed in such terms.
According to Freud (1976), the unconscious is the
primary psychical process, the secondary, or preconscious process being a later development. He
wrote (p. 763):

    ... the primary processes are present in the
    mental apparatus, from the first, while it is
    only during the course of life that the secon-
    dary processes unfold, and come to inhibit and
    overlay the primary ones; it may be that their
    complete domination is not attained until the
    prime of life. In consequence of the belated
    appearance of the secondary processes, the core
    of our being, consisting of unconscious wishful
    impulses, remains inaccessible to the under-
    standing and inhibitions of the preconscious,
    the part played by the latter is restricted
    once and for all to directing along the most
    expedient paths the wishful impulses that arise
    from the unconscious.

What we are also alerted to from the work of
Freud is the part that visual images play in reach-
ing the unconscious and in the reconstruction processes of memory. The relative immediacy of visual
images means that they can obtain a closer proximity
to the state of the unconscious than verbal information which stands at a higher level of coding.
Technically speaking, there is less need for transformation when information is presented in terms of
images. The immediacy of images, the symbolic por-
trayal of forbidden desires, and the irrationality
of the workings of the unconscious are central to
the work of Freud. We, as rational individuals,
may claim authority over our desires and impulses,
and yet if Freud is correct, we may, even in our
waking moments be subjected to unconscious motivations which are beyond our awareness, thereby exerting
influences of a subtle kind.

Below conscious awareness

While Freud's theorising has added an additional dimension to our appreciation of the motivational effects of drives which derive their purposes from levels which are below consciousness, his is not the
only source to which we can turn for explanations of
this kind. In fact studies of below conscious awareness can be found in the literature on perception
and in media studies, thus showing that there are
other dimensions to the problem. It would seem, as

The Importance of Motivation

Erikson (1958) suggested, to be preferable for the
term 'consciousness' to be restricted to a physiological interpretation relating to the degree of
alertness and activity of the organism, and for the
term 'awareness' to designate the psychological dimension. In the work of Koestler (1964) we find a similar position; he suggested that conscious and unconscious experiences do not belong to different compar-
tments of the mind, but form a continuous scale of
gradations, of degrees of awareness. This leads us
to consider the problem of persuasive communications
that are directed at a level of awareness which is
subliminal. The evidence for subliminal discrimination of stimuli appears to be negative, or at least
equivocal (Eriksen, 1958), but on the other hand
there appears to be substantial evidence that behaviour can be directed by above-threshold cues of which
the subject is not consciously aware (Rapaport, 1960).
Furthermore, as Rapaport went on to point out, experiments have been successful in demonstrating not only
the use of cues without the subject being aware of
them, but also the lack of awareness, in some instances, of the responses which he is making.
    The use of cues as a control device for influen-
cing responses, without the awareness of the recipient that such cues exist, has been a major finding
in television research (Baggaley and Duck, 1976).
Furthermore, cueing appears to be far more potentially persuasive than subliminal techniques, because
it can lend itself not only to control over sensory
emphasis, e.g. sound and vision, but also a variety
of non-verbal aspects of communication. For instance,
Baggaley and Duck found that camera angles and use
of notes by news presenters influenced the responses
of viewers. Such devices can be manipulated; they
are above sensory threshold, but they can be outside
conscious awareness; hence they can be employed as
devices for hidden persuasion. We shall see later
when we come to discuss semiological processes that
visual images carry the possibility of deception in
various ways, e.g. editing, focusing, lighting and
juxtaposition.

SUMMARY

1. Motivation can be generated by needs which may
    be innate or learned. Learned or secondary needs
    can be formed arbitrarily, for example by persu-
    asive communications.

2. The satisfaction of higher needs rests upon the
    continual gratification of lower needs. Lower

needs are always present, but they may exist in a state of latency.

3. Motivation may be employed in the strive for equilibrium, that is, towards a steady state; or it may be employed for the purpose of stimulation or arousal. Motivation may be employed in either direction, at different times.

4. The strength of motivational weighting rests not only upon the value placed upon the aim, but also upon the subjective probability of achieving the desired outcome.

5. Motivation can be explained, in some instances, in Freudian terms related to events below consciousness; or it can sometimes be explained in terms of 'below awareness', in which case it refers to subliminal events or cues which although perceptually present are not detected consciously.

REFERENCES

BAGGALEY, J. and DUCK, S. (1976) Dynamics of Television. Farnborough: Saxon House.

BERLYNE, D.E. (1960) Conflict, Arousal and Curiosity. New York: McGraw-Hill.

COHEN, A.R. (1964) Attitude Change and Social Influence. New York: Basic Books.

ERIKSEN, C.W. (1958) Unconscious processes. In Jones, M.R. (ed.) Nebraska Symposium on Motivation, vol. VI. Lincoln, Nebraska: University of Nebraska Press, pp. 169-227.

FEATHER, N.T. (1965) Performance at a difficult task in relation to initial expectation of success, text anxiety and need achievement. Journal of Personality, vol. 33, pp. 200-217.

FESTINGER, L. (1957) A Theory of Cognitive Dissonance. Evanston, Ill: Row, Peterson.

FREUD, S. (1976) The Interpretation of Dreams. Harmondsworth: Penguin Books.

GETZELS, J.W. (1964) Creative thinking, problem solving and instruction, In Hilgard, E. (ed.) Theories of Learning and Instruction. Chicago: The National Society for the Study of Education, pp. 240-267.

HEBB, D.O. (1949) The Organization of Behavior. New York: John Wiley.

" (1958) A Textbook of Psychology. Philadelphia: W.B. Saunders.

HOVLAND, C.I., JANIS, I.L. and KELLEY,H.H. (1953)
    Communication and Persuasion. New Haven:
    Yale University Press.
KOESTLER, A. (1964) The Act of Creation. London:
    Hutchinson.
MASLOW, A.H. (1955) Deficiency motivation and
    growth motivation. In Jones, M.R. (ed.)
    Nebraska Symposium on Motivation, vol. III.
    Lincoln, Nebraska: University of Nebraska Press,
    pp. 1-30.
MASLOW, A.H. (1962) Toward a Psychology of Being.
    New York: Van Nostrand.
McGINNIES, E. (1974) Cognitive and behavioural
    approaches to persuasion. In Silverstein, A.
    (ed.) Human Communication: theoretical explor-
    ations. New York: John Wiley.
MILLER, N.E. and DOLLARD, J. (1964) Four Fundamen-
    tals of learning. In Teevan, R.C. and Birney,
    R.C. (eds.) Theories of Motivation in Learning.
    New York: Van Nostrand, pp. 42-60.
PACKARD, V. (1962) The Hidden Persuaders.
    Harmondsworth: Penguin Books.
PACKARD, V. (1978) The People Shapers, London:Futura.
RAPAPORT, D. (1960) On the psychoanalytic theory of
    motivation. In Jones, M.R. (ed.), Nebraska
    Symposium on Motivation, vol.VIII. Lincoln,
    Nebraska: University of Nebraska Press,
    pp. 173-247.

Chapter Four

IMAGINATION AND THE FUTURE

Motivation, through the existence of desire, is
bound up with the future, a future which can be
grasped as a visionary experience, an experience to
which the expression imagination is given. Through
imagination, that which is absent can be made present,
and that which is desired can be possessed, figura-
tively speaking. Nevertheless, although imagination
is a visionary experience it does have its roots in
lived experience, a foundation which gives it an origin from which it can transcend and thus become
'other worldly'. This transcendence offers unlimit-
ed possibilities for thoughts or fantasies which may
bear no real connection with practical realities;
they may be self-generated without the intervention
of others, or they may be subject to the influence
of others. Man's imaginative consciousness provides
a ready-made vehicle or channel through which the
author can appeal in the propagation of his ideas;
likewise, it lays itself open as an avenue for those
engaged in the business of persuasion.
    The persuasion 'industry' utilises imagery in
many of its appeals, inviting its audience to project
themselves, via imagination, into some other state of
existence, or some other time or place. In doing so,
it feeds upon the potentiality of the imaginative
consciousness to transcend physical or practical limitations. In the earlier chapter on learning we saw
how behavioural controls or environmental situations
can be manipulated to influence human responses, but
there is more to persuasion than controllable situations, we need also to consider the place of imagination as a source of influence.
    The advertising copywriter, like the poet, can
conjure images through a particular choice of words,
while the producer of television programmes or advertisements has at his command a direct medium for image

44

making. Imagination offers a window to an invented future, and as in dreaming, it can give the appearance of making present that which is objectively absent. Advertisers often set out to encourage their readers/viewers to 'put themselves in the picture' or into a future with a brighter potential. It is only because imagination offers the possibility of transcending the present that such a technique possesses potency.

In the preceding chapter on motivation, we discussed the way in which drives or motives provide a basis for persuasive appeals; we now see how the same drives can be called upon as motivational sources for imagination, for example, imagining oneself in a prestige car (status), imagining oneself being welcomed into an admired group (affiliation). Because imagination allows the individual to conceive himself as otherwise, i.e. not held to present circumstances, it possesses an evocational element which can be used by advertisers in their bid to forge desirable connections with their products or services. The glamour side of commercial persuasion is replete with examples of appeals to imagination, and through imagination to a condition of self-transformation into a more ideal state, a state posited in the future. This borrowing of images was brought out by McKellar (1957), he was not writing about persuasion but his ideas are pertinent here. He wrote, 'To understand imaginative thought it is necessary also to take account of the fact that we can have memory images of the products of other people's imaginings.'

Other people's imaginings can be presented verbally or pictorially, and, of course, the choice will depend on the media available and the intention in mind. However, in terms of emotive power, it does appear, according to Koestler (1964), that visual images are more potent, hence the attraction of pictorial presentations in advertising. There is also the additional factor of immediacy; images are analogues, therefore they require less processing in terms of mental effort, the contrast here is between the digital (words) and analogue (images).

The reliance on visualisation for future recall can have its pitfalls, and it may be one of the reasons why pictorial advertisements appear to be so ephemeral. As McKellar (1957) suggested in reference to dream images, the predominance of visual imagery in dreams is probably one reason why they are so readily forgotten. It is, he suggests, easier to remember what has been verbalised, and as dreams pass from conscious awareness before any kind of sub-vocal verbalisation has taken place, we can appreciate why their contents may be transient. It could be argued that the same effect applies to the images which are received, for example, by the medium of television, this however is a speculative hypothesis which needs testing in some controlled way.

Future and magic

The importance of imagination for an understanding of persuasive communication lies in its potential for involvement with the future, its ability to connect, albeit in an illusory way, with that which is to be, or if not to be, then that which is desired. The possibility of unfulfilment is, however, ever present. In terms of persuasion, Berger (1972,p.146) noted the irony that 'Publicity speaks in the future tense, and yet the achievement of this future is endlessly deferred.' Of course it is not true to say that gratification is always endlessly deferred, it may be obtained in some instances and not others, one needs to be specific in making such claims. However, we can take the point he was making that publicity is often directed towards ideals which cannot be satisfied in any objective terms. But publicity will always speak about the future, the present and the past are not its concern.

The act of imagination underpins man's concern with magic; without imagination the concept of magic could not arise. Sartre (1972) saw the connection when he described the act of imagination as '... an incantation destined to produce the object of one's thought, the thing one desires in such a way that one can take possession of it.' Likewise, we can see the relevance of studies in mythology, particularly magic, for an understanding of certain advertising techniques. For example, Gossage (1967) shows the relevance of the concept of contagious magic to advertising; contagious magic is a process whereby it is believed that transference of a quality can take place from one object to another, or from one person to another merely by association, hence the term contagious. This, like all ideas of magic, requires the existence of imagination to make the necessary leap across the divide which separates the rational from the irrational.

To return to advertising, we can see many instances of the use of the concept of contagious magic, for example, the assumed transference through association of a particular quality of a well-known person to a branded product, or the placing of a product in a particular situation, usually a prestigious one,

for the purpose of gaining value. Many irrational
connections can be made either in the presented images or in the way that imagination seizes upon the
images; the parallel is with dreaming. In fairness
it should be pointed out that not all advertising
aims at the irrational, there are countless examples
of perfectly rational arguments or ideas being portrayed in advertising, particularly in the technical
press.

Distance and negation

The work of Sartre (1973) provides a valuable and
necessary framework within which we can find deeper
insights into the nature of imagination; being a
study in phenomenology it offers little in the way
of experimental evidence, but this does not detract
from the valuable insights which he presents. One
of the important distinctions which he makes is that
between perception and imagination; whereas both of
them deal with images, perception takes place in the
presence of an object but imagination is not so constrained. Imagination is, in Sartre's terms, at a
distance from the world; it is not connected by physical reality, although it may owe its existence to
some initial worldly experience. Moreover, imagination always refers to an absence, that which is present does not need to be imagined. So it is these
twin concepts of distance and absence that we find
of critical importance in understanding Sartre's
ideas of the nature of imagination. Once human consciousness, through imagination, is no longer tied
to that which is present, it can conjure that which
is not real or that which is absent.

Now let us look at the nature of images. We know
that we can have images of our own, for example, the
memory of a familiar face which can be recalled at
will, and we also know that we can be presented with
images in some mediated form. Sartre presented three
categories of images: (i) mental image, an image which does not require a material presence; (ii) port-
rait; (iii) caricature. The essential difference is
that the second and third images need a material presence. This difference has implications for imaginative constructions or reconstructions. A fully determined image presented externally for perception,
for example, a picture, may be so overdetermined that
it leaves little scope for imagination. Pre-formed
images stand as a kind of half-way house for consciousness, because they have substance, they are not
mental images but they can bear a likeness to such
images. Being analogical, material images possess

the more immediate potential of sliding into mental
images. This apparent immediacy (it is only apparent) makes them more emotive, it confers upon them
a kind of magical quality, an assumed reality. The
presence of a person is felt more strongly by a photograph of him or her than by a verbal description.
To allow for the play of the imagination when it is
presented with pictorial images, advertisements sometimes use the technique of deliberately blurring
parts of the image, one of the techniques is to have
parts of the picture 'out of focus'. This allows the
viewer to complete the picture through his own imaginings; it is as though psychological space is given
for personal evocation.

Imaginative consciousness

In imaginative consciousness the normal restrictions
of perception are set aside so that many points of
view can coalesce into a single whole. It bears
some similarity to Cubist art, without of course
having the constraints of artists' materials to contend with. The power of the imaginative consciousness is that it can visualise that which is absent,
it can construct images which need bear no correspondence to external reality, it can see things as
otherwise, and it can project itself to some future
condition, at least an envisioned future condition
(one can imagine going on holiday). This is a powerful potential that can be enlisted for a variety of
purposes, cultural, political or economic. It is a
condition to which persuasive communications, whether they be commercial in intent or propagandist, frequently address themselves. And it was towards such
conditions that Berger (1972) directed his thoughts
in his analysis of publicity images. The main weakness of Berger's position is that he equates all
publicity with exploitive motives, and he chooses
most of his illustrative examples from the field of
'glamour' advertising. This failure to distinguish
between different types of publicity is common to
many writers who seize upon advertising as an example of evils in the capitalist system. Advertising
itself is neutral, it is the purpose to which it is
put, and the techniques employed which should be the
object of value judgements. There are many technical
advertisements containing a large degree of factual
information; on the other hand, there are many other
advertisements which appeal to the irrational in man,
providing no facts, but feeding on the potential of
the imaginative consciousness to create the illusion
of personal transformation. In this latter context

Berger has a very good point, he detected a class
bias in personal transformations offered in advertising. He suggested that publicity addressed to the
working class tends to promise a personal transformation through the function of the particular product
it is selling (the Cinderella syndrome); whereas,
publicity addressed to the middle-class promises a
transformation of relationships through a general
atmosphere created by an ensemble of products (the
Enchanted Palace syndrome).

What is more important here is that it is man's
possession of an imaginative consciousness that makes
the whole process possible, so it is to the work of
Sartre that we must turn for deeper insights, and in
doing so we move to an acceptance, however grudging,
that the nature of man allows the possibility of persuasion to act upon imagination. In less gloomy
terms it was seen by Pascal as a kind of gift -
L'imagination, c'est le don de persuader les hommes.

Intention

One of Sartre's basic tenets regarding imaginative
consciousness is that it possesses intentionality;
that although it can be free-ranging, it obtains
resolution only through intention. This concept of
intention is perhaps one of the most powerful, if
not the most powerful, in the whole discussion about
persuasion, and it is central to the concept of imagination.

Intention is a kind of focusing device in the
imaginative consciousness, it concentrates and thus
it excludes; it is a selective device, selecting an
image to be raised into consciousness from a range
of alternatives. Without intention, nothing has
prominence, therefore one has to intend when one
imagines; for example, one only has a mental image
when one intends to put it there. Sartre gave an
illustration of the importance of intention for
imagination by reference to schematic drawings which
the viewer is called upon to complete or 'fill-in'
by the act of imagination. This 'filling-in' requires an intention on the part of the viewer to make
the necessary completion. In a more direct way, pictorial images, whether they are persuasive in intent
or otherwise, provide a particular focus and thus
they can be said to intend. They can provide 'food'
for the imagination, and this 'food' can be provided
by others with a particular intention in mind. Plays,
books and films all provide a kind of nourishment on
which the imagination can feed, the imaginations of
others can be the source of our own imagination, and

we often willingly and purposefully submit ourselves
to their influences. But, at the same time, the professional persuaders can also provide 'food' for the
imagination. Through the images of the commercial
artist and the words of the copywriter, illusions
can also be created, the same propensity of imagination can be seen as the core to which persuasive
appeals and literary works are directed. Koestler
(1964, p. 301) made the point in an interesting way
in relation to literature:

> Literature begins with the telling of a tale.
> The tale represents certain events by means of
> auditory and visual signs. The events thus re-
> presented are mental events in the narrator's
> mind. His motive is the urge to communicate
> these events to others, to make them relive his
> thoughts and emotions; the urge to share. The
> audience may be physically present, or an imag-
> ined one; the narrator may address himself to
> a single person or to his god alone, but his
> basic need remains the same; he must share his
> experiences, make others participate in them,
> and thus overcome the isolation of self. To
> achieve this aim, the narrator must provide
> patterns of stimuli as substitutes for the
> original stimuli which caused the experience
> to occur. This, obviously, is not an easy task,
> for he is asking his audience to react to things
> which are not there, such as the smell of grass
> on a summer morning. Since the dawn of civil-
> isation, bards and story-tellers have produced
> bags of tricks to provide such Ersatz-stimuli.
> The sum of these tricks is the art of literature.

Of course, the art of literature is more than the
sum of tricks, but the tricks that Koestler had in
mind relates to man's ability to conjure the presence of something in its physical absence. This is
man as symbol user, imaginative man, who has the
ability to give 'life' to that which is only symbol-
ically present, an illusory reality. The creation
of illusion for artistic purposes is part of man's
cultural heritage; it has its source in the imaginative consciousness, a source which also lies at the
heart of scientific endeavour. But the same source
which provides the origin of artistic and scientific
activity can be exploited by others for the purposes
of persuasion.
      It is only through imagination that we can
grasp the future, and it is because we can so project

ourselves, psychologically speaking, that we are able
to conceive ourselves as otherwise. However, the
otherwise that we desire to become may owe something
to the influence of others; who may be personal friends or acquaintances, or they may be idealized others presented through the various media. It is through these means that the commercial persuaders intervene, presenting for our consumption images of idealized selves, of selves that we could become. Although commercial persuasion may utilize man's gift of
imagination, what is has to offer is not a straight
gift, it is conditional, conditional upon the recipient of the message purchasing a commodity or service.
However, we need to guard against the simple assumption that people are pliant receivers of the contents
and intentions of all messages. Appeals to imagination are subjected to the censorship of practicality.
Most normal people are able to rationalise, and even
when appeals to irrationality manage to pass the
'censor of practicality', such appeals may produce
no more than a temporary illusion which is not translated into an overt act or response as desired by the
advertiser.

Conditioning and imagining

Before we pass on to the next chapter, we are now in
a useful position to make a contrast between persuasion directed towards conditioned learning of the S-R
type and persuasion directed towards imagination.
The contrast can be stated as the difference between
the effects of past sensory experiences working upon
present responses (conditioned learning) and the projection of mental images into a future context (imagination). The distinction, however, is not absolute,
imagination can utilise stored images, therefore, elements of the past can be a source of imaginative
projection into the future.

SUMMARY

1. Imagination rests upon the human potential to
    conceive negation or absence. The future is
    absence.

2, Through imagination, the future can be realised,
    psychologically speaking, in the present; thus
    it can be considered to possess magical propert-
    ies.

3. Imaginative consciousness is not constrained by
    perceptual awareness, but it does possess inten-
    tionality.

4. Persuasive appeals can provide external intentionality by focusing in particular ways.

5. Imagination is largely an activity of visual imagery, hence the importance of images in persuasive appeals directed towards imagined transformations of a personal kind.

6. Through imagination, ideas can be juxtaposed, and new associations created. This propensity can be utilised for persuasive or literary purposes.

REFERENCES

BERGER, J. (1972) Ways of Seeing. Harmondsworth: Penguin.
GOSSAGE, H.L. (1967) The Gilded Bough: Magic and Advertising. In Matson, F.W.and Montagu, A. (eds.) The Human Dialogue; perspectives in communication. New York: The Free Press, pp. 363-370.
KOESTLER, A. (1964) The Act of Creation. London: Hutchinson.
McKELLAR, P. (1957) Imagination and Thinking. Aberdeen: Aberdeen University Press.
SARTRE, J-P. (1972) The Psychology of Imagination. London: Methuen.

Chapter Five

THE MAKING OF SIGNS

Imagination makes it possible to visualise that which
is absent or to construct images which need have no
external reality. This ability is evident in man as
sign creator and sign user, exemplified wherever and
however man makes one thing stand for another, whether through the medium of speech or the variety of
artefacts at man's disposal.
     In this connection let us consider semiology,
the study of signs and sign-systems, as a discipline
in its own right. The study of semiology now forms
an essential component within communication theory,
and it has special implications for the study of persuasion. We have seen how environments can be controlled or manipulated, and now we must turn our attention to the ways that signs are constructed, and
having been constructed, the ways in which such constructions lend themselves to manipulation.
     The term sign can have two rather distinct mean-
ings, it may refer to concrete, material artefacts
like road signs, or it may refer to the mental process whereby one thing is associated with another,
for example, the mental link which connects a particular word with a particular concept. Both of these
meanings are central to our interest in persuasion,
we are interested in signs as artefacts in society,
and we are interested in signs as tools for thought.
     In persuasive communications the sign has spec-
ial significance, not only as a tool of thought but
also as a vehicle for the transmission of values in
society. Signs are made manifest in a variety of
ways, the most obvious example being speech or language itself. Other examples of signs are pictorial
images, gestures and other forms of non-verbal communication, and the many objects of material life
which are used to signify something beyond their manifest purpose. Their sign potential lies in their

expressive qualities. As a means of expression they
are signifiers, what they express is the signified.
The strength of relationships between signifiers and
signifieds is of fundamental importance to publicists
and advertisers in general, whose professional task
is the establishment, modification, and strengthening
of such relationships.

Codes and conventions

The establishment of relationships between signifiers
and signifieds, i.e. the creation of signs, is an arbitrary act which allows for the beginnings of codes
not only in the formal sense of scripted messages,
but also as social conventions. Here we can see persuasion directed towards the establishment, strengthening or modifying of coded relationships as part of
a cultural process, but in a direction carrying the
particular bias of the persuader.

Before we examine the persuasive potential of
signs, let us gain some familiarity with theoretical
concepts which can be used in our analysis, in particular we can borrow concepts from semiology. Semiology is concerned with codes and the rules of application of codes; hence it is concerned with the
way in which signification, that is, the correlation
between signifier and signified, is established and
utilised. Furthermore, it is because this correlation can be made in abstraction, without any necessary recourse to a referent, that important implications arise for persuasion. It is at this point of
signification or fusion between signifier and signified that possibilities for deception arise. Deception or lying have their ground in this condition,
a condition which rests upon the human propensity
to conceive a form of reality which has no basis in
observable fact.

It is this act of signification, the production
of signs as an act of cognition without any necessary
recourse to objective verification which is of special
importance to the study of persuasion. We shall note
that lying, i.e. the falsification of significations,
can be carried out via various communicational modes,
for example, verbal, non-verbal, graphical and pictorial. Moreover, it is possible for one communicational mode to be used to falsify another, for instance, the deceptive titling of newsprint photographs,
or the false smile accompanying a verbal utterance.
The ability to give signification, to conjoin one
thing with another in the absence of a referent plays
a major part in the processes of persuasion, and it
is reference to this condition which is missing in

theoretical studies of persuasion stemming from traditional psychology and social psychology.
     Having established the importance of signs as
mediators in the act or processes of persuasion, let
us look at the more formal developments that have
arisen within communication theory. One of the most
outstanding pieces of work relevant to our theme is
that of Saussure (a useful introduction to his work
is given by Culler, 1976) who emphasised the importance of studying the 'signs of society' under the
general rubric of semiology. He was concerned to
disclose the underlying systems by which meaning can
be transmitted, and this is also our concern, because
persuasion can be effected through different systems
of communication, verbal and non-verbal. We shall
find that by adopting a wider perspective of human
communication, and yet keeping it under the one rubric of semiology, important implications for the
study of persuasion are revealed. We find that we
are forced to attend to conventions and rituals, to
non-verbal practices of all kinds, and to view them
as systems much in the same way that language is viewed as a system. By directing attention to non-linguistic signifying systems, certain aspects that tend
to be hidden or covert in persuasion can be revealed.
In chapter seven a fuller analysis is made of the
general field of non-verbal communication and the
implications which it holds for persuasion.

Sign construction
A knowledge of how signs arise and how they function
plays an important part in the study of semiology.
Let us then take a closer look at Saussure's expos-
ition of the sign, remembering that in his terminology the word sign, unlike its general usage in the
English language, does not imply a physical entity,
it refers to a mental or cognitive event. It is the
fusion which takes place when an unvoiced sound image
becomes attached to a concept, for example, when the
sound in one's head, say chair, is associated with
the concept of chair. This then is the linguistic
sign according to Saussure; it is arbitrary because
basically there is no intrinsic relationship between
the two separate elements.
     The arbitrariness of linguistic signs means that
the world can be articulated in an infinite variety
of ways, and specific articulations to suit ideological or commercial objectives abound within the nature of language itself. The linguistic framework for
Saussure's theorising is shown in the following diagram (Fig.5.1),it illustrates the overall framework

of signification within which there are three separate but related terms. The first term in the diagram is signifier, this refers to the mentally heard sound image of a word; the third term, signified, refers to the concept evoked by the signifier; while the second or middle term, sign, refers to the mental relationship which fuses signifier with signified.

```
┌──────────┐                    ┌──────────┐
│signifier │       sign         │signified │
└──────────┘                    └──────────┘
```

Fig, 5.1 Linguistic framework of signification

The sign stands between and embraces both signifier and signified, it has no fixed property, but it serves to give meaning or more correctly signification. In figure 5.1 the diagrammatic representation is based on terms borrowed from linguistics, this gives a useful framework but it is not adequate for dealing with the non-linguistic aspects of communication. This framework can be extended in the way that Barthes (1977) developed his theorising on semiology. In the following diagram (Fig. 5.2) the form is the same as in the previous diagram, the difference being in the terms specified.

```
┌───────────┐                    ┌────────┐
│expression │      relation      │content │
└───────────┘                    └────────┘
```

Fig. 5.2 Semiological framework of signification

This terminology, which has its origins in the work of Hjelmslev (1959), widens the scope of possible interpretations. We can now move from linguistic considerations to a wider field of communicative events. We can include objects, images and all forms of non-verbal communication in the first term (expression). Regardless of terminology the sign is always a relationship not a fixed entity, except of course when the term is used in the practical sense of referring to some material sign-object, e.g. road sign, but even here there is an implicit symbolic relationship. As was stated earlier, the arbitrariness of signs allows them to be used as codes as part of the cultural process. On this basis, we can reflect on the importance of studying signs and hence semiology for the purpose of gaining further insight into the pro-

cesses of persuasion. We can set out to look for
the coded relationships within a particular appeal
or message, and we can note the particular cultural
codes which are utilised, remembering that the propensity to give meaning without any necessary referent in 'real life' carries the constant possibility
of deception.

Denotation and connotation

Man's sign-making propensity has important implications for persuasion, amongst other uses, it provides
the bases on which denotation and connotation are
formed and used for communicative purposes. Persuaders often denote a specific relationship between a
signifier and signified, for example, between a product name and a particular product or commodity. On
the other hand, persuasion may be indirect, alluding
without making explicit a relationship which it is
desired to evoke, for example, an advertisement may
denote a relationship between a named product, say
Lux, and cleanliness, but allude to sexual attraction.
This is connotation, the signification of secondary
or additional meaning to the one overtly stated or
denoted. Connotation, so to speak, uses the building blocks provided by denotation, relying on already
established relationships or signs. In the context
of society, such building blocks are given, in the
same way that words in a dictionary have established
meanings. From the store of denoted or primary meanings, the persuader has at his command a ready-made
resource for 'triggering-off' connoted or secondary
meanings.

Of course advertisers not only borrow existing
denotations, they often set out to give first meanings, to denote. This is particularly noticeable
when a new brand name identifies a new product. For
example, the linking of the brand name Biro with the
first ball point pens on the market. However, with
prolonged exposure and lack of initial competition,
the brand name may lose its status and become a gen-
eric name for a product, as in fact happened to the
word biro.

We can show in diagrammatic form the distinction
between denotation and connotation. Figure 5.3 illustrates denotation as a first-order or primary system, and figure 5.4 shows connotation as a second-
order system, borrowing the second term in denotation
(sign) and using it as first term or signifier. In
semiological terms, the notation is:

```
        Denotation:    E  -  R  -  C
        Connotation:   ERC -  R  -  C
```

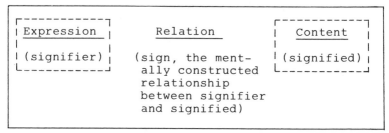

Fig. 5.3 Denotation, a first-order system (primary meaning)

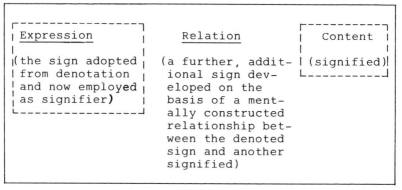

Fig. 5.4 Connotation, a second-order system (additional or extended meaning)

The collapsing of the planes of expression and content into the single term of relation or sign and its subsequent employment as a signifier, is a ubiquitous system, and it was seen as such by Barthes (1968, p. 90) when he wrote:

> Society continually develops from the first system (denoted) which human language supplies to it, second-order significant systems, and this elaboration, now proclaimed and now disguised, is very close to a real historical anthropology. Connotation, being itself a system, comprises signifiers, signifieds, and the process which unites the former to the latter,...and it is the inventory of these three elements which one should undertake in the first place for each system. The signifiers of connotation..

are made up of signs (signifiers and signifieds united) of the denoted system. Naturally, several denoted signs can be grouped to form a single connotator.

For example, a range of denoted signs, police helmets, double-deck buses, bowler hats, can coalesce to connote the general idea of Britishness. These then are the building blocks borrowed from society and used as a form of expression. The form of expression is the rhetoric, the way an idea is expressed, not the meaning of the expression.

When emphasis is placed on the way an idea is expressed rather than on the intended meaning, it can increase the persuasiveness of a message. As all messages have to be given form of one kind or another, they possess rhetoric. Seen in this light, rhetoric itself is part of the communication process, not some sinister addition. It is the intention behind the form of the rhetoric which we need to question when we suspect ulterior motives. It seems to be rather unfortunate that in everyday language the term rhetoric has gathered to itself a suspect 'ring'. In fact, a case could be made showing the positive aspects of rhetoric, for example when it stimulates interest or attention, or when it makes a message more memorable. Style and rhetoric share common ground, and when used in a creative way they may in fact change the way in which the content (signified) is taken into consideration; this of course is the intention behind persuasive messages of all kinds, be they commercial or propagandist. Whereas rhetoric is form, the form of the signifier, connotation is a system, a system which borrows signs from other systems for use as signifiers. This is the kind of second-order effect which we can observe in many forms of advertising, for instance, the use of pictorial images of well known personalities to signify additional meaning to the one overtly apparent in the product itself or in the name of the product. Many other examples can be found of the implicitness of connotation in advertising, e.g. for expensive cars (denoted) read status (connoted), for a clear complexion (denoted) read sexual attraction (connoted), Furthermore, concealment of the techniques employed in media production can present an illusion of a denoted system which may, in fact, be heavily connoted. It is to this problem of concealed connotation in production that we now turn, with particular reference to the use of pictorial images in message presentation.

Paradox of pictorial images

We have observed that connotation proceeds upon the basis of an established denotation which is 'set-up' without recourse to an existing code. However, the existence of these two levels of signification, one without a code (denotation) and the other with a code (connotation), can be a source of misinterpretation leading to the paradox of pictorial images being sometimes received as denoted, when in fact, they may be connoted. This arises from the fact that pictorial images being analogical appear to be natural and uncoded, when in fact the reality behind their existence includes interventionist devices which are not always apparent at surface level. Concealed treatment effects, detectable only to the experienced eye, can be considered as forms of coding, e.g. lighting effects, camera angles, focusing, editing, montage. By these various devices particular form is given to pictorial messages, with the intention to influence interpretation in a direction desired by the presenter. When treatment effects are undetected, pictorial images may be received unwittingly as bearers of authenticity because they appear to be natural and thus uncoded.

The apparent objective reality of pictorial images, their analogical qualities, gives rise to the paradox of coded and uncoded messages being carried inside one vehicle of representation. As Barthes (1977) suggested, this structural paradox coincides with an ethical paradox: when one wants to be neutral or objective, one strives to copy reality meticulously, as though the analogue, in this case the pictorial image, is value free. And yet we know that in practice this is not so, camera angles have to be selected from a range of alternatives, thus there exists an arbitrary component from the outset. Additionally, the milieu in which programmes are constructed combines to produce effects which are connoted, that is, relying on primary codes; thus the milieu also serves a semiotic function, and being semiotic carries the possibility of deception, a deception which can be used for persuasive purposes. Barthes work is of particular relevance to the analysis of pictorial methods of communication; he dealt in detail with the semiotic implications of the photographic message, in its static form as print and in its moving form as film.

The core of Barthes' theorising rests upon the distinction between the analogue and the digital in human communication. Analogical representations are those that bear a 'likeness', e.g. photographs and

graphic illustrations, in contrast to the digital
mode which bears no resemblance to its reference,e.g.
words. The analogue is borne on a continuous scale
without discrete boundaries, whereas the digital is
discrete and therefore discontinuous in scale. Another important distinction is that analogical representations while displaying a reduction in proportion
to their reference do not undergo a transformation in
the mathematical sense of the word, in contrast to
the digital which always involves transformation thus
detaching itself from perceptual 'reality'.

As stated previously, the pictorial image contains the paradox, within itself, of possessing analogical qualities which are 'readable' across cultural
boundaries and treatment effects which are subject to
coding. Moreover, the 'reading' of pictorial images
ia also subject to historical factors, which can also
be employed in the coding of messages. These coding
devices are often employed in persuasive appeals in
which images are taken from past events and placed
in the context of the present. In addition to this
borrowing of images from the cultural past there are
the technical devices of retouching of photographs,
contrived juxtaposition of images, selection of particular camera angles, and editing, all of which can
combine to produce a particular interpretation.

We have looked at the pictorial image, and we
have noticed that it offers the potential for deception, a deception which is all the more powerful
because it is carried on the basis of analogical properties which seem at surface level to be uncoded,
and therefore, not subject to cultural intervention.
However, we should extend our analysis to include
the interaction between text and photograph, a condition common to many commercial advertisements.

The linguistic component in an advertisement
carrying both text and illustration serves to direct
the reader to particular signifieds; in other words,
it acts as a kind of control device which cues the
reader into a pre-chosen path of signification, at
least that is the intention. To use manipulative
language, it remote controls the reader to a chosen
meaning. Advertisements possessing text and illustrations (pictorial or graphic) possess three distinguishing characteristics:

      (i) a denoted image, that is, they bear a like-
          ness to what they desire to represent,
          they are analogues;

     (ii) a connoted image, that is, the image its-
          elf is subject to treatment, and thus

produces second-order inference or signification;

(iii) a linguistic message, the accompanying
text which anchors or guides the reader
towards desired interpretations, those
intended by the advertiser.

Potentials for persuasive effects are offered
by each of these characteristics. The apparent naturalness of the denoted image can give the illusion
of a message without a code. The treatment of the
image can be concealed, at least to those people not
familiar with the techniques, thus allowing the image
to appear as being denoted, when, in fact, it is connoted. The linguistic message accompanying the image
or illustration can guide the reader towards particular interpretations, acting as a kind of route marker through a chosen path of connotation.

The influence of the various effects which we
have discussed rely upon the propensity of the human
mind to give signification without external verification, the media themselves as signifying systems
can be organised in such a way that preferential or
persuasive signs can emerge. What we need to be
alerted to is not only the treatment effects which
can be used to elicit particular meanings, but the
borrowing of already established primary meanings,
the codes of society, and their usage as vehicles
for connotation. When we say, as we will do more
forcefully later in this book, that propaganda talks
the language of the people, what we shall mean is
that propaganda feeds upon the meanings or more correctly the significations that are already established
in society, that is, it utilises existing codes. How
do codes work upon people; do people always come to
the same idea when given identical information through the codes of society? This is a question we
need to go into more thoroughly, in order not to
make the error of assuming that the significations
presented by the media effect a uniform interpretation and response.

SUMMARY

1. Signification is founded upon the relationship
   between signifier and signified. This is the
   foundation for codes and social conventions as
   codes.

2. The arbitrariness of signification lends itself
   to the possibility of deception and falsification.

3. Denotation establishes codes, connotation utilises established codes.

4. Pictorial images, static or moving, may appear natural or uncoded, when in fact they have been subjected to treatment effects which render them coded.

5. The text accompanying illustrations acts as a route marker, guiding the reader towards intended meanings, i.e. value is provided.

REFERENCES

BARTHES, R. (1968) _Elements of Semiology_. New York: Hill & Wang.
BARTHES, R. (1977) _Image, Music, Text_. London: Fontana.
CULLER, J. (1976) _Saussure_. London: Fontana.
HJELMSLEV, L. (1959) _Essais Linguistiques_. Copenhagen: Nordisk Sprog-og Kulturforlag.

Chapter Six

THE PROBLEM OF MEANING

Meaning is fundamental to the whole process of persuasion, without meaning there is only incomprehension.
In the last chapter we were concerned with signs,par-
ticularly the sign produced by the act of cognition,
and we saw that it can be constructed without any
external referent; this is the ground of signification, of human thought and its potential for abstraction. In contrast, meaning can be derived empiric-
ally though experience gained from the world, thus
providing an additional source, if not the primary
source of meaning. On the one hand we are dealing
with semiotic man, man as sign and code user, and on
the other hand we are dealing with pragmatic man,
man related to events and objects in the world. Of
course, the two cannot be neatly separated in the
life of the person; practical events influence thought,
and signs and codes likewise influence thought. In
this chapter, a particular interpretation of the nature of meaning will unfold, but first of all let us
take a look at some conjectures about the concept of
meaning from other relevant fields of enquiry.
    Wilden (1977) writing on communication makes a
clear distinction between meaning and signification;
to him, meaning is conveyed in the form of analogue
while signification is conveyed in digital form. In
other words, signification bears the hallmark of a
code, being a system of category differences, whereas
meaning is fluid, not distinguished by boundaries.
In the language of communication theory, the distinction is between the continuous (analogue) and the
discontinuous (digital). This distinction has attraction but fails to take account of the fact that
the analogue can be subjected to treatment effects
which render it less transparent. For example, as
we discussed in the last chapter, it is possible to
modify pictorial images in a way which conceals the

treatment; this can be considered a form of coding
and thus the apparent innocence of the analogue is
lost. Therefore, meaning without the infiltration
of signification is unlikely to be achieved in mediated communication, it belongs more to man's relationship to the natural state.

As distinct from communication theorists, lin-
guists define the concept of meaning within the framework of language itself, for example, Leech (1974,
p. 9) wrote:

> Meaning can best be studied as a linguistic
> phenomenon in its own right, not as something
> outside language. This means we investigate
> what it is to know a language semantically,
> e.g. to know what is involved in recognizing
> which sentences are meaningful and which are
> not ... that point presupposes a distinction
> between knowledge of language and knowledge
> of the real world.

The distinction here of course is between semantics
which deals with the significations found in words
and pragmatics which deals with words in relation
to their practical consequences and contexts.

Ideas can be taken from other sources to give
us a wider frame of reference for the concept of
meaning. For example, in the field of philosophy
Langer (1976, p.55) stresses the formation of relationships as lying at the base of meaning; and writes,
'its (meaning) essence lies in the realm of logic
where one does not deal with qualities but only with
relations.' This idea of relationships is the central clue; but signification is also based on the
formation of relationships, as we found out when
discussing signs and their composition in the last
chapter. Signification and meaning both arise from
the mental or cognitive act of connecting one thing
with another, the difference in Wilden's terms lying
in the source of the material from which the connection is made, digital in signification and analogical
in meaning. However, in the final analysis, meaning
or the giving of meaning is always the act of a person, but it also has social overtones. Meaning can
be accumulated from real, world referenced events or
objects, and then translated into significations
whose authenticity may go unchallenged. Signification then becomes equivalent to meaning and herein
lie the seeds of magic.

States of conditional readiness
Another avenue for us to follow is that of information

theory. Information theorists (Shannon and Weaver, 1949) viewed communication as a process or transaction between terminals, a process of generating and reproducing symbols, and they paid no attention to the problem of meaning. This lack of concern with meaning and concentration upon the techniques and mechanics of communication is understandable in the context of the origins of information theory which arose within the field of telecommunication engineering. For the telecommunication engineer, the problem was one of achieving maximal potential from equipment, which meant in practical terms achieving as many communicational links as possible on a single physical channel. The actual message or at least its contents was of no concern to the telecommunication engineers or information theorists.

In such a theoretical climate the work of MacKay (1969) had its origins, a highly technical climate, but one which opened up whole new avenues for theorising on communication and psychology, from which concepts such as channel capacity, redundancy, information load, and 'bits' were to follow. However, the concept of meaning was left aside until MacKay brought it into focus within the general framework of information theory; although his terminology is couched in the technical language of information theory, he conceded the importance of including reference to mental or cognitive states. In his terms meaning is the selective function performed by a message on the recipient's state of conditional readiness for goal-directed activity. This is a functional interpretation of the concept of meaning, but makes concession to motivation, a factor not included in information theory.

To grasp the concept of meaning as a functional or organising activity, one needs to visualise a computer which has been programmed to work within a particular language and with particular routines; these set the limits to is function and the possibilities of its internal organisation. It has its restrictions, and so has the human brain, which has physiological limitations and psychological limitations.

The ideas that MacKay put forward are of vital importance to our theme. To illustrate the concept of meaning he gave an analogy with a railway shunting-yard, the shunting-yard being analogous with the human brain. At any given moment, he said, the configuration of levers in the box defines what the yard is ready to do to any waggon that happens to come along. The levers have certain possibilities and no more; so the controller has to make selections, and any one

choice gives a particular meaning in the situation.
In terms of the human factor, the production of meaning rests upon two elements, firstly the framework
of the individual's cognitive state, and secondly
the determination or selections made within this
framework. This concept of meaning is operational
or organisational, operational because it is seen in
active terms and organisational because it is concerned with the ordering or patterning of thought. It
is not to be found in external stimuli, but such stimuli can act upon the human brain to cause it to ali-
gn or order itself in a particular way, and this is
the meaning. The form of the message acts upon the
cognitive state of readiness to receive information;
it makes a particular selection, and this particular
selection is the meaning.

The key concepts of MacKay's work on meaning
could be summarised as follows:

(i) conditional readiness - the range of
states that are available for processing
information, in other words, the cognitive
state of the recipient, i.e. the resources
available for thinking;

(ii) selective function - what a message actually achieves in terms of causing the
brain to orientate itself in a particular
direction, this is only possible within
the conditional state of readiness
mentioned above;

(iii) intended meaning - the selective function
that the sender of a message intends to
take place in the brain of the receiver;

(iv) effective meaning - the interpretation
given to the message by the receiver;

(v) conventional meaning - the norms set by
society, it has statistical properties,
i.e. it is norm referenced;

(vi) misunderstanding - when a mismatch occurs
between intended and effective meaning.

The 'lock' and the 'key'

We have concentrated upon meaning as it is created
in the mind or the brain of the receiver of a message,
but how about the meaning intended by the sender of
the message? Is there a difference here? And how
about meaning in society? We need to give attention
to these questions because communication is inevitably bound up with them, and so is persuasion. For

the sender of a message, the meaning of his message
is the selective function which he wants it to per-
form on the receiver's cognitive state. This can be
quite different from the effect it actually performs,
this is the effective meaning as distinct from the
intended meaning; and both the intended meaning and
effective meaning may differ from some standard or
conventional meaning.

We can utilise MacKay's concepts for considering
not only the effect of messages, but also the effect
of advertisements and indeed any stimulus which is
intended to act on the thoughts of others. All communications are sent with intent, the intent to cause
a particular set of ideas to arise in the thoughts
of the recipient, in the terminology of MacKay, to
select from a conditional state of readiness. Such
a process can be visualised as a key (the message
itself) and a lock (the cognitive state of the receiver). A key is only viable when it fits a lock, likewise a message has to be designed to fit a mental complex. The originator of a message has the double task
of envisaging the cognitive state or complex of the
receiver, and of designing his message in such a way
that it makes the correct selection within that state,
i.e. it achieves the desired orientation within the
limitations of the receiver's particular cognitive
framework. Metaphorically speaking, the sender has to
forge a key which is appropriate for a particular lock.
For intended meaning to realise itself as received
meaning, it follows that a message originator has to
utilise a code (language) which is shared by himself
and the receiver, and to operate with concepts which
already have some bases for attachment or expansion.
There is a parallel here with metaphors, words which
although out of context in current discourse carry
links for the creation of new meaning. To return to
the computer analogy used earlier in this chapter,
the originator of a message can only ensure the mat-
ching of his intention with received meaning when he
utilises the recipient's 'computer'. When his language or code differs it is his responsibility, not
that of the receiver, to make the necessary modifications to ensure that the intended message is received as such. Of course, by a programme of re-education it is possible to make the receiver capable of
receiving a new code or language, and this is what
formal education is often directed towards.

The act of communication possesses two distinctive features or functions, its intended function and
its interpretative function. When sender and receiver
share the same mental constructs they tend to respond

in a similar way to a message or event. However, as
MacKay pointed out, it is possible with a different
pattern of past experience,or a different set of
goal-priorities for one person to have evolved a mental construct of the world beyond the conceptual grasp of another person, such that two individuals do
not have the same perceptual experience when confron-
ted with the same stimuli.

Meaning and persuasion

The concept of meaning as an organising process
rather than a fixed entity residing in some property
has important implications for a general theory of
persuasion. Persuasive appeals are more likely to
be successful when they are made with full cognizance of the conceptual frameworks of the persuadees,
and when they are couched in codes (languages) familiar to them. That such an awareness is present
can be gauged from the form or rhetoric of newspapers which tend to reflect the language styles and
concept levels of their readership.

Talking the 'language of the people' is one of
the noticeable attributes of propaganda. Propaganda,
as Ellul (1973) suggested, does not create new material or beliefs, it establishes common bonds between
sender and receiver, but at the level of the lowest
common denominator in order to reach as wide an audience as possible. Fest (1977) outlined very clearly
the planned way in which Hitler in Nazi Germany play-
ed upon ideas and latent beliefs already existing in
the German nation. Not only do propagandists 'talk
the language of the people', they also tend to omit
controversial issues, thus avoiding the 'mismatch'
which can occur when the sender and receiver do not
share the same cognitive framework. For immediate
comprehension and acquiesence in accepting the goals
of a message, the propagandist has to take account of
the terms and conditions in which life is perceived
and understood by his audience.

The idea has been put forward here that meaning
is an ordering or functional activity, that except
for conventional meaning which bears statistical properties based on norms of usage, meaning is not to
be found but to be constructed. It is derived from
the perception or conception of relationships, this
is always an activity of the individual, and as such,
it is open to idiosyncratic constructions. In any
instance of communication, meaning can differ between sender and receiver, this can lead to misunderstanding, and it can negate the purpose or intention
of the communicator or persuader. Of course, when

sender and receiver are in a face-to-face relationship, other cues are generated which give extra information, but this information is often of an emotive kind, giving the receiver additional information
about the sender's attitude or feelings. The main
vehicle for attempting influence or persuasion in
society is natural language, and as we shall see in
the next chapter it contains within itself two distinct attributes, firstly, it is a tool for conceptualisation, its rational role, and secondly, it is
a means of generating feeling, its emotive or affective role.

SUMMARY

1. Meaning can be of three kinds: (i) intended
    meaning (by the sender); effective meaning (by
    the receiver); conventional meaning (by society).

2. Apart from conventional meaning, meaning is not
    found, it is established. The relationships
    are the meaning.

3. In operational terms, meaning is the selective
    function or discrimination carried out on the
    individual's cognitive state of readiness.

4. Messages can be likened to keys opening avenues
    of thought, and like keys they have to be des-
    igned to fit an existing complex, the complex
    of the receiver's mind.

5. To be effective, communication and persuasion
    has to operate within the constraints of mean-
    ing outlined.

REFERENCES

ELLUL, J. (1973) Propaganda. New York: Vintage Books.
FEST, J.C. (1977) Hitler. Harmondsworth: Penguin.
LANGER, S. (1976) Philosophy in a New Key. Cambridge,
    Mass.: Harvard University Press.
LEECH, G. (1974) Semantics. Harmondsworth: Penguin.
MacKAY, D. (1969) Information, Mechanism and Meaning.
    Cambridge, Mass.: The M.I.T. Press.
SHANNON, C.E. and WEAVER, W. (1949) The Mathematical
    Theory of Communication. Urbana, Ill.: Univer-
    sity of Illinois Press.
WILDEN, A. (1977) System and Structure. London:
    Tavistock.

Chapter Seven

THE DIFFERENT FACES OF LANGUAGE

So far we have reviewed a number of building blocks
in the construction of an inter-related theme of persuasion. The importance of relationship was paramount; we saw this in the discussion on learning, on
remembering, on imagining, on sign-making, and on
'the giving of meaning'. Relationships may be of a
spatial or temporal kind as implied in behavioural
conditioning, or they may be mediated, in which case,
the forms of mediation are of special concern to us,
because the forms themselves can possess persuasive
potential, or rhetorical power.
    Of the various forms of mediation employed in
human communication, the most vital is that provided
by natural language, i.e. the language acquired in
childhood in a non-formal way. Unlike formal languages, such as computer languages, natural language
possesses expressive qualities which lend themselves
readily for use as persuasive devices. As a medium
of communication, natural language serves two distinct
roles:
          (i) as a means for conceptualisation, its cog-
              nitive role; and
         (ii) as a means for conveying or generating em-
              otion, its affective or emotive role.

    Stress, intonation and pitch are natural in spe-
ech, and they provide clues to intended emotive meanings or values. In passing, it is interesting to note
that in printed language attempts are made to convey
qualitative meanings by the use of such devices as
bold type and italics. What we can discern in speech
is that it possesses in one vehicle of expression
both the digital and the analogue; digital because
it conveys words as discrete categories, and analogue
because it displays magnitudes of difference, e.g.
pitch and intonation. This dual capability is of

special significance to our work, because it will be
found to provide a subtle link with studies in attitude formation and attitude change, an area of crucial significance to persuasion.

Persuasion is invariably directed towards either
the formation, strengthening or change of people's
attitudes. Here the term attitude is used to cover
both the cognitive and emotive aspects of knowing or
awareness. And it is in this connection that natural language with its potential for expressing concepts and feelings can be seen to have special significance. As a medium of communication it can be used
to persuade in a rational way, as for example when
one is influenced to purchase a commodity on the basis of newly acquired technical information. Or it
can be used in an emotive way, appealing to desires
which have no basis in rationality. It may however
display a blend of rationality and emotion, and this
is a task for which natural language is well suited.

Rational and non-rational
Although a positive statement has just been made
about the two directions of persuasiveness which
exist in natural language, we can find in studies of
the ethics of language that the term persuasion is
limited to one aspect of language, namely the non-
rational. In fact, Stevenson (1944) was quite explicit in proposing that rational arguments are to be
clearly distinguished from the persuasive, that non-
rational arguments appeal to the value or emotive
factor and that they are invariably accompanied by
non-verbal features which heighten emotion without
adding to the logic of the argument. This is a particular definition of persuasion, implying a change
in attitude, but not through the exercise of logic.

As a medium of communication natural language is
not an ideal vehicle for achieving degree zero of persuasion, it is not an easy task to separate the rational from the non-rational, the logical from the
emotive, nor to deliver the spoken word in such a way
that the surrounding non-verbal accompaniments are
neutralised and thus lose their persuasiveness. As
Stevenson suggested, natural language militates against a pure emotive or pure rational appeal, because
it contains few words which only have an emotive meaning. We find that the nature of language is such
that relatively few arguments are wholly persuasive,
in terms of them being non-rational, and few are
wholly rational. In oral discourse, voice quality,
pitch and modulation add dimensions which cannot be
easily neutralised except by a process of careful

self-monitoring.

Vagueness in language

Metaphors provide a good example of the possible intertwining of the rational and non-rational, they
permit a vagueness which enables them to carry cognitive and emotive potential within the one framework. The steps by which metaphorical links are established may be forgotten, and a logical connection
which is initially implied may appear as natural.
They may have been used so often that sender and receiver cease to be aware that the words are not literal. For example, one may speak of the 'sifting of
evidence' without raising to consciousness the process of sieving wheat from which the metaphor has its
origin.

Natural language itself is richly endowed in metaphors which possess extensive embedding in the roots
of language, roots which extend to man's practical or
lived experience. The naturalness of the origins of
language become transmuted into forms of expression
which are symbolic, a symbolism which can conceal
their identity or at least keep their identity sus-
pended in a state which is normally below the level
of consciousness. In sucn cases, the figurative
becomes the literal.

The liberal use of metaphors can be analysed in
terms of symbolic transformations, and attention can
be directed towards the way in which such transformations open the possibility for the compression of
thought into fewer units, with the ever present possibility that such compression can facilitate a leap
across the gap of rationality. Thus metaphors may
serve to compress thought rather than widening it as
required in logical reasoning where explanations are
expected at each step in thought without borrowing
from other systems. We can see here a link with myths
in the sense that myths and metaphors both rely on the
transmutation of cognitive or emotional experience.
Cassirer (1973, p.26) saw it as a symbolic transformation of a basic mental activity, with myths and language being two diverse shoots of one basic process.

Natural language is not neutral, it bears the
marks of its history through metaphors and styles of
usage. The problem of neutrality in language is a
particular focus in the work of Barthes (1977a). He
contends that the personal factor of style or crafts-
manship and the social codes from which language is
constructed combine to shape or influence the form
of messages, and that this can take place without the
conscious awareness of the writer. Thus the medium

itself imposes an effect which clouds any attempt of absolute transparency in communication between sender and receiver; it carries the historical weight of its usage in society and the finger prints of each individual communicator. In scientific discourse, however, natural language tends to carry fewer metaphors, emotive words are eschewed, and the ordering of the communication is designed to appeal more to logic than emotion.

Notwithstanding the attempts in scientific discourse to aim for rational presentation of ideas, we are still faced with the fact that in everyday language emotional elements are invariably intertwined with rational elements. Human reasoning, whether it is about decisions, opinions, beliefs or values, cannot entirely divorce the two elements of rationality and emotionality (Eco, 1977). Persuasiveness of a non-rational kind persists in natural language, particularly so in the ethical use of words. Ethical language, words used to convey concepts related to value judgements, of duty and moral obligations, of feelings towards things, people and events (like 'duty' and 'ought', 'good', 'bad', 'right', and 'wrong') appear not to carry information in terms of knowledge or beliefs, but to convey manner or to exhort. Stevenson addressed himself to the latter in discussing ethical language and persuasion. He gave the following example of the use of ethical arguments in the heightening of suggestibility (p.141):

1st person: 'It is morally wrong for you to disobey him.'

2nd person: 'That is precisely what I have been denying.'

3rd person: 'But it is your simple duty to obey him. You ought to obey him in the sheer interest of moral obligation.'

In this example the terms duty, ought, and moral obligation do not provide any additional information in terms of fact, but because they are ethical terms they carry a persuasive influence. It is possible to interpret such language as possessing influence only on the basis of common or shared knowledge of social commitments or responsibilities, it rests upon implicit knowledge which does not need restating on each occasion. It is when people do not share a particular factual background and yet are faced with moral imperatives to which they cannot relate that resentment can arise, and persuasive language of this kind can meet resistance.

In developing the theme of ethical language

and its usage we can turn to the work of Wellman (1961) who contended that the vagueness or coarseness of language can, at times, be a distinct advantage. For example, it would be inappropriate to use an adjudged clinically accurate language at times or in situations where there is no commensurate precision of analytical thought or conceptualisation. A practical example could be the use of words borrowed from the language of statistics to give a kind of respectability to the interpretation of data which may not warrant such finesse. Wellman went on to claim the advantages of the imprecision of ethical language in the following way (p.301):

> If ethical language is imprecise, this is because of the limits of our ability to discriminate the various degrees of value and obligation. The vocabulary of ethics will express accurately every distinction of value and obligation we are capable of making... If there were an ethical language which was less vague, we should be unable to make use of it, for we are incapable of reaching any definite judgements in these borderline cases. The language we do have is quite adequate to formulate the insight we actually possess.

But how about the ethical problem of moulding attitudes? If we consider that it is legitimate to mould attitudes, then it would appear that ethical language would be an important means of carrying out the task, but its success would in part rest on implicit knowledge. However, this does raise the moral issue of the aims, circumstances, and methods which are acceptable, so we come full circle to the ethical problem, not merely of language usage, but intention underlying the usage. And it is in the intention behind all forms of persuasive communications that the resolution of the value, positive or negative, of persuasion lies. For example, one may feel that it is morally correct to publicise art exhibitions but not bull fights, depending upon one's own particular moral standpoint. People can be quite selective in their use of ethical language, they may sanction it in situations of social control or influence, while frowning upon its usage in more obvious exploitive instances, such as in commercial advertising. Given these qualifications, ethical language itself is quite legitimate, assuming that in the act of communication the sender and receiver possess the same or similar frameworks for interpretation.

Language engineering

Language can be fabricated for the purpose of achieving specific intentions or manipulations. Perhaps
language always has a manipulative intent (see Mac-
Kay's ideas discussed earlier), but according to
Leech (1974) it can be carried out in two ways (a)
by conceptual reshaping, the rational use of language involving logic and denotations; and (b) associative engineering, the use of words with affective
associations, and drawing upon connotations. These
two categories are complementary to the rational and
non-rational categories which we used earlier in this
chapter and it is the problem of making neat category
distinctions of this kind which makes assessment of
persuasiveness of language less than straightforward.
    Of particular interest is the presentation of
quasi-logical proof masquerading as logical proof.
Very often propaganda is presented in a form which
is analogous to logical proof with connections or
associations being made which owe more to the emotive
aspect of the communication than to the rational or
logical side of argument. The effectiveness of such
techniques can only be gauged by reference to the
attitudes or responses produced in the audience, and
this will depend on the efficiency of the message to
cause meaning by making the desired selection from
each individual's cognitive state of readiness. It
is well known from the work of Hovland (1957) that
the educational level of message recipients plays an
important part in the acceptance or otherwise of a
particular message; the better educated the audience
the less disposed they are to be influenced by non-
rational arguments, particularly when contrary views
are not presented. One needs more than knowledge
of the construction or engineering of language for
an analysis of its effects. The work of Packard
(1962) is a useful example of an uncritical acceptance of the power of media or language manipulators;
he presented or exposed some of the principles employed in message construction, but he gave little
evidence of the effects in terms of behavioural responses or attitude change. What we can discover of
course is the structure or 'engineering' of language,
from which inferences can be made about intent.

Advertising language

We shall now focus upon the specific use of language
in advertising. According to Leech (1966) who made
a detailed study of the use of language in advertising, such language can be classified under the general heading of 'loaded language', i.e. language

directed towards change in attitudes with particular emphasis upon the emotive or non-rational side. But a more extensive appraisal would make further category distinctions or differences within the whole field of advertising; for example, it would be more sound to give weightings to the different forms of advertising, to the technical press and national press, and even here, category differences can exist. For instance, advertisements in a prestigious newspaper like The Times tend to differ from those in a more popular newspaper like The Sun. However, although a great deal of advertising language may be 'loaded', advertisements themselves tend to be overt, displaying themselves for what they are, in sharp distinction to propaganda which tends to be covert. Mayer (1958) who had much to say in a negative way about the whole profession of advertising, did concede that it 'displays its wares openly'. And we can find a similar echo in the writing of Barthes (1977b, p.33):

> ... in advertising the signification of the image is intentional; the signifieds of the advertising message are formed 'a priori' by certain attributes of the product and these signifieds have to be transmitted as clearly as possible. If the image contains signs, we can be sure that in advertising the signs are full, formed with a view to optimum reading; the advertising image is frank, or at least emphatic.

In this example, Barthes was addressing himself to the visual images used in advertising, and hence this is more of a semiological point than one of linguistics; nevertheless, the same intention of identity with the advertised product can be found whether the message is verbal or visual.

The context in which advertising is placed is perhaps the most important determinant of its specific character. We usually find that advertisements in the popular press employ a more colloquial style of discourse, being more informal and making greater use of imperatives; while in the 'status' press and in specialised journals the style tends to be more formal. However, whatever the media, copywriters are prone to stating only one side of an argument, the side they choose is nearly always the positive one showing no blemishes, only good points. On the face of it this would appear to be the most effective technique for generating favourable attitudes in their readers, but as we know from the work of

Hovland mentioned earlier, this is not necessarily the most productive way of influencing others. With more discerning people (better educated was the term used by Hovland) it is often advantageous to present two sides of an argument, and hence gain credibility for the totality of the message.

It could be argued that such stylistic differences reflect an underlying social difference in the use of language, and that copywriters merely attune their copy to suit circumstances. As the work of Bernstein (1973) shows, within the framework of one common language, namely English, there exist marked stylistic differences. These stylistic differences are echoed in the daily press, and it could be argued that this is a commercial recognition of an underlying social condition.

In this chapter we have been dealing with language as a tool possessing persuasive potential; it possesses the power to influence by logical argument, or by appeals to the non-rational or emotive part of man's mind. However, when persuasion is studied within the field of the ethics of language, it is only the latter, the non-rational, which is deemed to be persuasive. While disagreeing with this restricted interpretation of persuasion, we can appreciate the emphasis placed on non-verbal features as contributory agents in the process of persuasion exemplified in the work of C.L. Stevenson. In the next chapter we shall take a closer look at these features.

SUMMARY

1. In the language of ethics, persuasion is regarded as a non-rational way of altering attitudes; while here, it is suggested that both rational and non-rational methods can be considered to serve persuasive purposes.

2. Ethical language rests on tacit understanding of shared values and obligations; its persuasive power is reduced when sender and receiver do not share the same common values.

3. The imprecision of ethical language is a reflection of the imprecision of values themselves.

4. Metaphors provide an example of the intertwining of the rational and non-rational in natural language.

5. Advertising tends to be explicit, declaring itself for what it is.

6. Stylistic differences in media language can be accounted for in terms of assumptions held about the language styles of their readership.

REFERENCES

BARTHES, R. (1977a) Writing Degree Zero. New York: Hill & Wang.
BARTHES, R. (1977b) Image, Music, Text. London: Fontana.
BERNSTEIN, B. (1973) Class, Codes and Control. St. Albans, Herts: Paladin.
CASSIRER, E. (1973) The Power of Metaphor. In Maranda, P. (ed.) Mythology. Harmondsworth: Penguin,pp.23-31.
ECO, U. (1977) A Theory of Semiotics. London: Macmillan.
HOVLAND, C.I. (ed.) (1957) The Order of Presentation in Persuasion. New Haven: Yale University Press.
LEECH, G. (1966) English in Advertising. London: Longmans.
LEECH, G. (1974) Semantics. Harmondsworth: Penguin.
MAYER, M. (1958) Madison Avenue, U.S.A. Harmondsworth: Penguin.
PACKARD, V. (1964) The Hidden Persuaders. Harmondsworth: Penguin.
STEVENSON, C.L. (1944) Ethics and Language. New Haven: Yale University Press.
WELLMAN, C. (1961) The Language of Ethics. Cambridge, Mass.: Harvard University Press.

Chapter Eight

NON-VERBAL EFFECTS

In our discussion on language as an agent in the
process of persuasion, we have seen that in communication the verbal is closely intertwined with the
non-verbal, particularly when language is used to
express emotion. We are also intuitively aware of
the emotive and hence persuasive effects of, for
example, facial expression and gesture in the many
types of social encounters which bring people into
face-to-face relationships. Furthermore, we can note
that the contrived reality of theatrical, cinematic,
and television productions relies primarily upon non-
verbal signs for the display and dispatch of emotion.
It can be said that non-verbal communication helps
to quicken and heighten emotion. It is not only the
acting profession that sets out deliberately to convey emotion by these means; politicians also stage
manage their performances. An extreme example of
this is the way in which the German Nazi Party stage-
managed their annual rallies at Nuremberg (Fest,1977).
But to a lesser extent the annual political conferences of political parties in western democratic
countries also display the same trait of stage-managed performances heavily accentuated with rhetorical flourish.
    Generally speaking, it is the rhetoric, not the
content, which provides the most immediate effect.
The rise and fall in speech tone and the dramatic
gesture punctuate and compel, and in so doing they
provide an indication of the speaker's emotive involvement with the contents of the communication, not
only the speaker's emotive involvement, but also the
desire which he possesses for his audience to be
similarly involved.
    We may seek to disentangle the verbal from the
non-verbal for study purposes, but in normal social
interaction non-verbal communication takes place

within a context which includes language and the
wider framework of cultural conventions. Because
human communication can involve verbal and non-verbal
elements within the one interchange, it is possible
for discrepancy to appear between the two systems.
However, what appears to be clear is that when there
is discrepancy between what is said and how it is
said, it is the non-verbal which provides the more
trustworthy comment to the message (Bateson, 1973).
The precedence accorded to non-verbal signs when
there is conflict between the verbal and non-verbal
means that this can be used for deception or dissemblement, and hence induce a form of hidden persuasion. People voluntarily submit themselves to a
form of benign deception when they watch plays or
see films, and it is in these situations with all
the nuances of the non-verbal that emotion is heightened. In the performing arts the non-verbal component adds something additional to the narrative,
here the actor has at his disposal a number of non-
verbal parameters. By modulating these parameters
a plenum of meaning can be portrayed (Miller, 1972).
    The use of non-verbal devices is persuasive to
the extent that attitudes are modified, and the degree to which we are open to such modification can at
least be intuitively felt by the degree of transformation that we, as viewers, undergo in the theatre or
cinema, or in the face of a televised play. It becomes apparent that whether we are in 'stage-managed'
or in real life situations, the influence of non-
verbal signs is an important determinant of our
attitudes towards particular situations, events or
people.
    We are all well aware that the theatre is a
place for the dramatisation of the human condition
and that, for communicative purposes, there is a
need to exaggerate gesture and other non-verbal elements. On a similar, but reduced scale, it is possible to conceive that in everyday life a parallel
process is enacted; that life itself when people are
in the presence of others is a dramatic process. The
work of Goffman (1970, 1974) maintains that we can
in fact interpret social interaction in such dramatic terms. It can be seen that individuals do manage the impressions they give to others, firstly by
what they say, which Goffman termed expression 'given',
and how they say it, meaning of course the variety
of non-verbal signs, which he termed expression
'given-off'. Goffman's concept of impression management through control over the expression 'given-off'

is closely related to dissemblement as mentioned
earlier, and as the work of Ekman and Friesen (1973)
shows, the detection of false or dissimulated non-
verbal signals is an important step in avoiding their
persuasive effects.

In addition to the deliberate intent to deceive
by the use of non-verbal signals, misinterpretation
may also arise from discrepancy appearing between
intention and interpretation, that is, between what
the sender intends his message to mean and what the
receiver actually interprets the message to mean.
To illuminate this point we must return to the work
of MacKay (1969) and to his concept of goal-directed-
ness in human communication, in particular we find
in his later work (MacKay, 1972, p.24) a clear enun-
ciation of differences in interpretation when goals
are incorrectly perceived. Figure 8.1 illustrates
the four basically different categories of a situation which can emerge when non-verbal signals are generated.

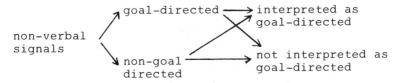

Fig. 8.1   Differences in interpretation

What we can see from this illustration is that
intended (goal-directed) non-verbal signals may
achieve their objective or they may be neutralised
by lack of awareness of their intention. On the
other hand, a situation may arise whereby a sender
may display non-verbal behaviour which is not intended as part of a communicative act, but nevertheless
it may be interpreted as possessing intent or meaning. In terms of persuasive influence, we can see
the possibilities of 'misreading', that is, non-verbal
signals possessing no persuasive power when it is intended that they ought; on the other hand, they may
possess persuasive power when they ought not, i.e.
when no intention on the part of the sender exists.

The modifications imposed on the verbal by non-
verbal factors are of central importance in the study
of human communication and, by inference, the study
of persuasion. As a specialised field of study, non-
verbal communication can be approached from the atom-
istic level, focusing on constituent elements such
as gesture and facial expression. Such an approach,

which is common to most of the literature in this
field, carries with it the aura of scientific respectability because of its attachment to experimentation and statistical analysis, but it may often
leave the reader in some ignorance of the wider theoretical framework in which non-verbal communication
can be embedded. In particular, we need to be aware
of the analogical nature of non-verbal communication,
and the importance this has for the creation of meaning as distinct from signification.

Relationship between verbal and non-verbal
Lyons (1972) proposed a schema which provides a
useful classification for the various properties
surrounding spoken language and their inter-relation-
ship in the overall features of conversational interaction. Two major categories can be distinguished,
namely 'prosodic' and 'paralinguistic', providing
frameworks for a range of other non-verbal components
or elements. Here the term prosodic is used to cover
the various elements of spoken sounds, i.e. intonation, stress, rhythm, pitch, voice quality; the term
paralinguistic covers the non-sound elements which
are supportive of verbal communication, i.e. gesture,
head movement, facial expression (including eye contact), and posture. The following table gives some
impression of the way in which the two factors can
be plotted against speech (verbal characteristics),
attitude, and the regulation of conversation. It is
the attitude related characteristics which are of
special importance to our interest in persuasion.

	Speech related	*Attitude related	Regulation of conversation
PROSODIC (speech sounds)	intonation stress rhythm pitch voice quality	intonation stress rhythm	intonation rhythm
PARALINGUISTIC (non-sound, but support- ive of speech)	gesture head- movement facial- expression	gesture head- movement facial- expression	gesture head- movement facial- expression

* This refers to the idiosyncratic and culturally
acquired features which express an individual's
attitude in a particular context.

Fig. 8.2 Functional characteristics.

Although the table shows the prosodic and paralinguistic features as separate entities, they are not necessarily mutually exclusive; they can also serve in supportive roles to each other, e.g. word stress (prosodic) may accompany gestural stress (paralinguistic) in particular instances. An example of this could be hurried rhythm of speech accompanied with amplified gesture, rhetorical devices expressing the attitude of the speaker.

When we consider the regulation of conversation we can also note the importance of prosodic and paralinguistic features, for example, change in intonation may be used to indicate the relinquishing of conversational turn, and gesture or eye contact may serve the same purpose. The opposite effect can also be obtained when paralinguistic features are employed to suppress conversational turn-taking. We have observed that paralinguistic features are supportive of speech, however, we may also observe that certain features, e.g. gesture, facial expression, and posture, may be employed as preliminaries to vocalised interaction. They may act as 'early warning devices' suggesting the type or style of interaction which is to follow, thus serving a metacommunicative function. In assessing the place of these various non-verbal features in conversational interaction, or in any situation where people are in face-to-face relationship, it is necessary to bear in mind that cultural differences may influence or modify the ways in which they are employed or interpreted.

Analogical properties

Technically speaking, all forms of information transmission and processing systems that rely upon discrete elements, for example, binary codes or lexicons, are digital systems. Words are discrete elements which define concepts. Elements of a particular concept are bounded within a set on certain referential or categorised bases. The digital mode of language prescribes and delimits, its linguistic function is primarily the sharing of nameable information, its overall function is the transmission or sharing or reproduction of pattern and structures (Wilden,1972).

Because digital systems employ discrete elements, for example, words with discernible boundaries, they lend themselves to coding, but this is not the case with analogue systems. The process of digitalisation creates a higher level of organisation than is found in analogical representation, it is more arbitrary and therefore less connected in its form to the ideas which it represents. This greater distance between form and content makes digital representation more flexible as a medium of communication, but what it gains in terms of signification is offset by loss of emotion. The difference is between the text of a written or printed message and the same text delivered as an oration.

Briefly, the essential characteristics of the digital mode of communication could be listed as follows:

(a) existence of discrete elements marked by gaps and boundaries between elements;

(b) concern with signification;

(c) differences marked by distinctions and oppositions;

(d) a higher level of organisation, therefore, a lower logical type than analogue;

(e) less dependence on proximity;

(f) arbitrary, therefore a suitable source for codification.

Having outlined the distinctive features of digital communication, we shall now take a closer look at the properties of the analogue which underscores non-verbal communication. The first and major distinction is one of scale; digital is discrete, that is, it is based on distinctive steps, whereas analogue is non-discrete and continuous, it shows as 'more' or 'less' and is characterised by relationships. Many other logical distinctions can be made, for example, digital is abstract and analogue is concrete. Analogue systems communicate by displaying continuous relationships; differences are those of magnitude and gradation, whereas, digital systems communicate distinctions in terms of sets, concepts, and binary states.

The combination of digital and analogue finds useful expression in spoken language. The abstraction of language is given an 'image of reality' through the continuous gradations which issue forth through the various prosodic and paralinguistic features, such as intonation, gesture and facial expression. The sensation produced by the analogue may provide no additional logical information, but it does add something to the message, and as we saw when we discussed the language of ethics, this something is regarded as being potentially persuasive. We have been mainly concerned here with spoken language, but as Wilden (1972, p.164) pointed out, poets employ devices such as alliteration in order to evoke analogue sensations even though the words on the page are digital.

A picture now emerges of human communication possessing two complementary properties which differ in emphasis according to whether communication is made through speech or print. The sensory manifestations of communicative acts are analogical, but their cognitive references, i.e. concepts, words, are digitalised abstractions. Generally speaking, the two modes are complementary and reinforcing, for instance, important words in speech are usually accompanied by a greater amount of prosodic and paralinguistic emphasis. The orator uses all the available non-verbal devices to give form to his message, and in 'playing' upon the form, he can deceive by underplaying the content. The style itself can become persuasive, or in Goffman's terms, expression can be managed for strategic purposes. This management refers to control over the verbal and non-verbal, but contradiction can arise in such a situation, and when it does this raises what is technically known as a problem of cross modality (Austin, 1967). However, as the work of both Bateson (1973) and Lyons (1972) shows when there is contradiction between a verbal utterance and its associated prosodic and paralinguistic features, it is these latter, non-verbal factors which help to determine the status of the verbal, i.e. whether the utterance is a question or statement, or whether it is a command or request. The precedence accorded to the non-verbal in classifying or typifying communications gives it a special role, a role as an agent of metacommunication.

Message labelling

Metacommunication refers to the nature of the communication not to the content; for example, the statement 'I want you to take this seriously' bears no content information, but it is, nevertheless, a communication. Metacommunication is of a different logical type than the message to which it refers, and according to Bateson (1973) we rely mainly upon prosodic and paralinguistic features, such as intonation, facial expression, and gesture for its expression. In normal communication, correspondence exists between message labelling, the metacommunicative component, and message content; for example, a message containing serious content is normally accompanied and prefixed by an appropriately serious facial expression. When this is not the case, when there is conflict between metacommunicative label and message content, a condition of perplexity can result;

such a condition, when intensified over a period of
time without being resolved, can lead to the pathological state described by Bateson as a 'double-bind'.
    The detection, conscious or unconscious, of non-
verbal signs plays a significant part in the correct
assignment of metacommunicative labels. Mode falsification, the artificial laugh, simulated friendli-
ness, and the like, can be identified and checked
against verbal content for veracity. This search
for cues in the non-verbal sphere plays an important
part in the detection of disguised persuasive influences. This leads us to consider the types of cues
which are generated in social encounters or interactions.
    At the present time we are still a long way from
defining all the subtleties of cues which are generated during speech and conversational interaction.
Nevertheless we are aware, often subconsciously, of
their existence. The literature on the subject of
the micro-elements which contribute to the macro-
structure of non-verbal communication is quite extensive. Of particular interest is the work of
Birdwhistell (1973) who analysed body movement (technically known as kinesics); the work of Hall (1963)
who analysed interpersonal distance (technically
known as proxemics); and the work of Argyle (1975)
and his co-workers on eye contact and gaze.
    However, serious problems arise in the attempt
to codify the separate aspects of non-verbal communication. The problem could be attributed to the
analogical and intuitive bases of non-verbal cues
and their strong attachment to cultural conventions.
This latter condition could account for the cross-
over effect which we saw in figure 8.1 with reference
to the work of MacKay which illustrates the way in
which non-verbal signals may be interpreted as intended when in fact they are not intended, and vice
versa.
    Non-verbal cues may serve three separate functions:

   (i)   they help to frame and label messages,
        that is, they serve a metacommunicative
        function;

  (ii)   they provide indexical information, that
        is, they give information about the speak-
        er, his attributes and attitudes;

 (iii)   they help to regulate conversation by
        providing cues for turn-taking, turn-
        relinquishing, and turn-suppression.

From these three functions implications arise of a persuasive kind: firstly, at the metacommunicative level, labels can be assigned, metaphorically speaking, which serve the purpose designated by the sender in order to achieve a particular effect, this could be achieved by mode exaggeration or by mode falsification; secondly, at the indexical level, personal clothing can, for example, 'give-off' impressions or suggest attributes and thus be part of impression management. The third function, that of conversation regulation, has less obvious implications for persuasion, but in terms of involvement and commitment through involvement it will be seen that turn-taking cues have a part to play in encouraging such behaviour.

Sources of non-verbal communication

Let us look at three specialised areas of research into non-verbal communication, i.e. facial expression, gesture, and voice quality. Of the various forms of non-verbal communication, the face is the most important for signalling emotional states. Research in this area has concentrated upon three inter-related aspects: (i) the general configuration of eyebrows, eyes, and mouth; (ii) eye contact; and (iii) gaze, i.e. the length of time that eye contact is maintained. The face can express a wide range of emotions, from joy to sorrow, and from pleasure to anger. It may reflect personal or interpersonal attitudes, and it is a source of feedback providing cues for the continuation, interruption or termination of social interaction. Control over facial expression tends to be more carefully monitored than control over other aspects of bodily communication (Ekman and Friesen, 1973),with the exception that micro-momentary expressions, lasting approximately 1/5 second, tend to escape the control of the speaker and thus, when detected by the listener, can provide indication of attempted deception.

Gestures also express emotion, in addition, they provide intensity to points requiring special emphasis. They are used to punctuate speech, and when an audience is at a distance where facial expression is hard to detect, they supply an additional source of information. There are of course national and indeed regional differences in gestural action, and this needs to be borne in mind when assessing the form or rhetoric of non-verbal communication. Furthermore, one must always bear in mind that non-verbal communication is markedly context bound, what is taken for an intended communicative gesture in one context may have no such significance in another.

Facial expressions and gestures provide visual information, but the sound or quality of the voice in the act of speech production is another source of information for influencing what is being said. It can, with practice, be used to infer status, to give credibility and thus be an agency of persuasion. Mehrabian (1972) studied the persuasiveness of voice, and he found that people who spoke faster, louder, and at a more regular speed were perceived to be more persuasive. However, we might add that there is a distinction between being perceived to be persuasive and being actually persuasive. For the latter, some indication of change or strengthening of attitude is necessary.

The implications of non-verbal communication for the study of persuasion are extensive; for instance, it has been shown (Argyle, 1975) that emotive messages have more effect than rational ones, and that non-verbal signs are strongly supportive of the emotive content of messages. This provides some support for the work of Stevenson (1944) discussed in the previous chapter on the contribution of non-verbal elements to the persuasive, non-rational side of language.

The precedence accorded to the non-verbal when contradiction arises between the verbal and non-verbal attests to its power in communication. This power appears to lie in its analogical properties, its concreteness and ability to induce relationships, as Wilden (1972, p.164) wrote,

> ... the politician may ... be apparently conveying denotative information about issues and events when in fact he is actually talking about his relationship to his audience and their relationship to the image and images he projects. ... This is in essence the prime distinction between the function of the digital and that of the analogue. The digital mode of language is denotative... its linguistic function is primarily the sharing of nameable information... The analogue on the other hand talks only about relationships. In human communication there are often serious problems of translation between the two.

In this chapter we have dealt with non-verbal aspects of communication, and we have noted the way in which the non-verbal supports the verbal, particularly by providing emphasis and emotive intensity. To this extent it can be seen to possess a particular quality which is directed towards the non-rational aspects of persuasion. We have also noted that non-verbal features can be used to give impressions, impressions which can be used to deceive. In particular, we have stressed the importance of the non-verbal as an analogical form of representation in contrast to the verbal which is digital. In the next chapter we shall go on to consider a wider non-verbal issue, namely the place of symbolism and the part it plays in persuasion.

SUMMARY

1. Non-verbal signs add an analogical dimension to speech.

2. Non-verbal signs may support the verbal, on the other hand, they may be contradictory, in which case they tend to provide a more trustworthy commentary, except in instances of dissimulation.

3. Non-verbal signs can serve a metacommunicative function, indicating the nature of a communication.

4. Attributes may be ascribed to speakers on the basis of the non-verbal features which they display. Therefore, control may be exercised over these features in order to secure a desired effect.

5. Non-verbal signs may be read as intended, on the other hand they may not. Cultural and contextual differences have a bearing on interpretation.

6. The face is more closely observed than any other part of the body, but it is also more carefully controlled by the addresser, thus it is more likely to be used in attempted deception.

REFERENCES

AUSTIN, W.A. (1967) Non-verbal communication. In Davies, A.L. (ed.) Language Resource Information for the Culturally Disadvantaged. Champaign, Ill.: National Council of Teachers of English.
ARGYLE, M. (1975) Bodily Communication. London: Methuen.
BATESON, G. (1973) Steps to an Ecology of Mind. St. Albans: Paladin.
BIRDWHISTELL, R.L. (1973) Kinesics and Context. Harmondsworth: Penguin.
EKMAN, P. & FRIESEN, W.V. (1973) Non-verbal leakage and clues to deception. In Argyle, M. (ed.)

Social Encounters. Harmondsworth: Penguin, pp. 132-148.

FEST, J.C. (1977) Hitler. Harmondsworth: Penguin.

GOFFMAN, E. (1970) Strategic Interaction. Oxford: Blackwell.

GOFFMAN, E. (1974) The Presentation of Self in Everyday Life. Harmondsworth: Penguin.

HALL, E.T. (1963) A system for the notation of proxemic behavior. American Psychologist, vol. 65, 1003-1026.

LYONS, J. (1972) Human Language. In Hinde, R.A.(ed.) Non-Verbal Communication. Cambridge: Cambridge University Press, pp. 315-344.

MacKAY, D.M. (1969) Information, Mechanism and Meaning. Cambridge, Mass.: M.I.T. Press.

MacKAY, D.M. (1972) Formal analysis of communicative processes. In Hinde, R.A. (ed.) Non-Verbal Communication. Cambridge: Cambridge University Press, pp. 3-25.

MEHRABIAN, A. (1972) Non-Verbal Communication. Chicago: Aldine-Atherton.

MILLER, J. (1972) Plays and players. In Hinde, R.A. (ed.) Non-Verbal Communication. Cambridge: Cambridge University Press, pp. 359-372.

STEVENSON, C.L. (1944) Ethics and Language. New Haven: Yale University Press.

WILDEN, A. (1972) System and Structure. London: Tavistock.

Chapter Nine

SYMBOLIC INFLUENCES

We have seen the part that non-verbal signs play in
human communication; in particular we saw how the
non-verbal adds a persuasive dimension, how it adds
stress to the emotive aspects of communication, and
how it can provide metacommunicative labels which
inform the receiver about the nature of the communication. In our search for the roots and processes
by which persuasion is effected, we need to turn to
the wider forms of non-verbal communication in society, forms which may accompany or often supersede
the verbal. In our quest we turn to symbolism as a
unique form of human communication possessing strong
persuasive potential.

In earlier times symbolism tended to be confined
more to religious practices and other ritual forms
of behaviour, but with the growth of industrialisation and the greater range of possibilities for producing artefactual images, symbols of greater variety have become more prevalent. The marketing of
products has taken on a symbolic role, goods have
come to be identified with symbols, for which the
term 'branded' is appropriate. With the branding of
commodities and the rise in advertising, the task of
marketing has, in some respects, become one of selling 'images', which has brought in its train a kind
of deification of certain products. A situation has
been created whereby people are encouraged to buy
products for their symbolic value, or, if not solely
for symbolic reasons, then for a symbolic addition
to the purely functional. The work of Berger (1972)
makes interesting reading in this connection. Symbols
and symbolism in the form of ritual behaviour have,
historically, provided powerful sources of persuasive
influence. The long historical traditions of some
symbols, for example, the snake and the lion (Saxl,
1970) testify to their potency as agents or metaphors

through which humans can represent aspects of their condition, and simultaneously make available another resource for influencing others.

As was mentioned in the earlier chapter on language, metaphorical connections may become obscured or blurred, and thus what is initially a symbolic connection can come to take on the appearance of being natural. This collapsing of the symbol into a form of psychological reality is interesting in two ways: (i) it demonstrates how the past can take on a living present, the basis of mythology; and (ii) how images can be projected into an imaginary future, carrying with them the full weight of emotive associations. Symbols may be employed overtly or covertly, their origins may be clear and explicit, or they may be lost in antiquity. They may be denotative, prescribing and informing, or they may be connotative, implying but not specifying. Symbolism pervades our lives in many diverse ways, for example in art, in literature, in religion, in ritual activities, in commerce (through advertising), in politics, and through politics to propaganda. Symbols, when they are employed as labelling devices usually have a rational intention; but on the other hand, they may be employed in a non-rational way, evoking but not explaining; it is in this sense that we shall be looking at symbols for their persuasive import. We shall also refer to the instrumental nature of symbolism as a means of expression; in this respect we shall be identifying ourselves with work in social anthropology. A practical example is the flag, as a symbol which may be a rallying point for group action (Firth, 1973), and thus carry a strong persuasive potential.

The persuasive power of symbols, whether they be images as symbols or ritual behaviour as symbols, rests upon their ability to evoke particular associations. However, when the associations are obscured by history, the symbols may produce merely ritualistic responses which are more representative of the ethos of a culture than the chosen responses of the individual. At a deeper level, and if we subscribe to Jung's (1964) perspective on symbols, we may interpret symbols in the primordial sense as being representations of an inheritance of a collective unconscious; but this perspective, although interesting in its own right, is outside the brief which we have set ourselves in this study.

In general, studies of symbolism have tended to emphasise the lack of natural links between symbol and referent, to refer to the symbol as being conven-

tional and arbitrary rather than natural and motivated (Firth, 1973), this is the classical meaning of
symbolism, a meaning which takes the symbol as a
concrete indication of an abstract value. However,
in the case of iconic symbols some degree of motivation is seen to exist, because the symbol, in this
instance,bears some degree of likeness to the thing
it represents; in other words it is an analogue.

These views about the nature of symbolism, while
interesting in their own right, are not particularly
helpful in explaining the way in which symbolic associations are made and subsequently utilised in the
process of persuasion. We need to know something
about the conventions or codes which form the bases
of the associations which sustain symbolism. Conventions and codes shape interpretations in many
ways, they affect interpretation of artistic forms
(Gombrich, 1962), and social life in general.

Mythology

The forms of codification that we are looking for
in terms of symbolic influences, and in terms of our
interest in persuasion, are exemplified in mythology.
According to Barthes (1973), myth is a mode or form
of signification, it is a semiological system, therefore, it can detach itself from external reference
and be self justifying. This potentiality can serve
a number of purposes, but the most important one
from our point of view is that it can be a language
that talks about itself, but only in borrowed terms.
It borrows its terms from an existing order. This
is the first-order of denotation that we met when
we discussed the making of signs in chapter 6. You
will recall that connotation utilises the sign produced by denotation as a signifier, thus connotation
is a second-order system. Likewise, myth makes the
same kind of borrowing, it is also a second-order
system; it is illustrated in the following way (see
figure 9.1):

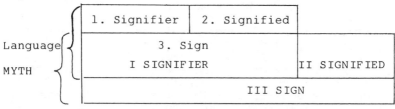

[from Barthes, R. (1973) Mythologies,
p.115, reprinted with permission]

Fig. 9.1 Language and Myth.

From the illustration it will be seen that myth rests
upon an existing language, therefore it is a second-
order system. But the important point for us to note
is that this language need not be linguistic in the
formal sense as a language involving words. It is
a language in the wider sense as a means of expression. Instead of words, the language of mythology
can be constructed from artefacts in society, which
then form the basis of a semiological chain in the
same way that words provide the source material in
verbal language. Barthes used the term language-
objects to describe the units of mythology, and it
is language-objects of all kinds that man can draw
upon to speak about his condition, and in speaking
about his condition he gives signification, and thus
enters the realms of abstraction. It is this abstracting, this talking about a condition via the use
of language-objects that gives mythology its power.
It is here that form and meaning can become confused,
the form or the style can be the meaning. This is
possible because the form of the myth is made up of
elements from another primary source, it rests upon
some previously established order. In other words
there is a kind of historical borrowing of shared
artefacts or events, which then form the basis of a
new language, the language of mythology. It is a
language created from the history of a society. So
it comes about that shared images can take on mythological potentiality, that is when they are used as
forms which have been hallowed by tradition. There
is a kind of concealed attenuation between form and
meaning, thus they can be confused.
  We can now relate this information to the purposes of this study, because persuasive communication
of all kinds can borrow images already existing in
society and turn them to their own purposes. The
stock of images historically accumulated in society
provide a ready-made source of signifiers, and as
such they possess both meaning and form. It will be
seen that this opens the possibility for the duplicity of the signifier, that is, it can carry 'meaning'
from a first or denoted system, and 'form' from the
second system. And when the signifiers are iconic
an even greater potential for duplicity can be manifest, because as analogical devices they are more
motivated, and therefore closer to 'meaning' than
'signification' in Wilden's (1977) terms as discussed
in the earlier chapter on meaning. The important
function of myth is the transformation of history
into culture. It transforms meaning into form, and
it is through form or style that images can receive

the treatment which may betray their persuasive intent. The form takes on meaning and the meaning takes
on form; when we focus on either of these two conditions separately we are not deceived, that is when we
read the image or myth for what it is. However, if
we obscure the difference between meaning and form,
we are likely to be influenced by the myth (Barthes,
1973).

Naturalisation of the symbolic
The attempt to convey as natural that which is symbolic pervades many advertising messages, particularly
in pictorial advertisements, carrying as they do the
deceptive possibilities of the iconic or the analogue.
Generally speaking, such advertisements carry a surface level innocence which can be at once beguiling
and persuasive. It is the unsuspected conjoining of
form and meaning, the naturalisation of the symbolic
or cultural that allows it (mythology) as Barthes,
(1973, p.131) wrote:

> ... it creeps, so to speak, through the back
> door of Nature ... this is why myth is exper-
> ienced as innocent speech, not because its in-
> tentions are hidden, if they were hidden, they
> could not be efficacious, but because they are
> naturalized...what allows the reader to consume
> myth innocently is that he does not see it as
> a semiological system, but as an inductive one,
> where there is only equivalence, he sees a kind
> of causal process: the signifier and signified
> have, in his eyes, a natural relationship...
> any semiological system is a system of values;
> now the myth consumer takes the signification
> for the system of facts: myth is read as a
> factual system, whereas it is but a semiological
> system.

This naturalisation of the symbolic is a fact
touched upon in a slightly different manner in the
work of Leach (1976). In describing the difference
between symbols, signs and signals, he went on to
demonstrate the way in which arbitrary associations
(which he termed symbolic) can, with repeated presentations, come to appear as intrinsic rather than
extrinsic as required by symbols, this implies a kind
of naturalisation of the symbolic, a naturalisation
filled with ambiguity. Persuasive messages may be
constructed in full knowledge of this condition, they
may obscure the arbitrary or symbolic connection and
present an impression of a 'natural' or intrinsic

condition. Here the historical use of language and
language-objects with their established denotations
can be called upon to provide culturally generated
'meanings' which, in semiological terms are merely
significations. Or in Leach's terms, symbols may
become signals; what in the first place is purely
arbitrary may become conditioned in the Pavlovian
sense; the non-natural relationship may become nat-
uralised. The symbolic is now reality.

Persuasion, when it operates through mythology
and ritual, rests on the potential for the symbolic
to be transformed by a mental process into an apparent reality. The human propensity to confuse the
symbolic with the 'real' is observable in many manifestations of human activity, it is observable in
religious practices, in theatrical viewing, and
indeed anywhere that symbols generate emotive responses. This attenuation can also have the effect
of causing a kind of 'double-think', a kind of sim-
plification which eschews contradiction and dial-
ectics, thus operating on a surface without depth.
And it is this mode of operation that we can notice
in much of advertising and certainly in propaganda;
facts are usually given without explanation and contradiction is avoided, life is positive and choice
is kept to a minimum because choice itself may require explanation.

The propagandist, when he constructs his message,
uses language, ideas or objects which are already
in the possession of his audience; a first-order
system of signs are at his disposal which he can
use as a metalanguage. The historical intentions,
which lie ready to hand, can be utilised by the
propagandist in the formation of his message, what
is arbitrary can be delivered as though connected
by some 'natural' law, meaning and form can be in-
verted, rhetoric can be taken for substance. It can
be likened to a conjuring trick in which reality is
turned inside out; history is depleted, to be con-
sumed by nature. Thus, deliberate manipulations of
messages can conceal the historical determinations
of the signs and symbols from which they are composed, in consequence a false curtain of 'naturalness'
may be accepted as reality. What the receiver needs
to do is to distinguish between meaning and form,but
for persons not versed in the technical means of
media production, or the origins of the ideas presented, such a distinction is not easy to detect.
The inextricable binding of form and meaning in analogical or iconic representations makes them ideal
vehicles for persuasive intentions; one has to make

a deliberate effort to focus on the form, and even so, there is a tendency for the mind to reverse and to focus on the meaning; in psychological jargon, it is a 'figure ground effect'.

The strength of analogical representations in providing meaning is demonstrated by the use of photographs in the press, here the unsuspecting reader may not be aware of all the various manipulations which have contributed to the form. For instance, the initial choice of picture, the selection or emphasis of particular detail, the retouching, the choice of half-tone screen, and the actual positioning of the photograph in the newspaper or journal, all may contribute to the sum total of effects which may go unsuspected by the reader. Not only in the press but also in television similar manipulations are employed by programme makers (Baggaley & Duck, 1976). Here we must refer back to the concept of denotation, as a first-order system which does not rely on an existing code, and it is at this level of denotation that the photograph or television image receives its apparent objectivity; it is here that they can be seen as messages without code. And because of this concealment of treatment effects which allows a connoted message to be received as denoted, illusion can be created. Thus we can observe the connection with mythology, it is apparent in the way that images are borrowed from society, images which have been hallowed by tradition, and by the intertwining of form and meaning. The closer the relationship between the form and the idea portrayed, the greater is the possibility of illusion, hence we can see the power of the analogue or icon for generating meaning in the sense of actuality, and with it the greater possibility of emotive responses. Witness the reverence for religious sculptural forms and the emotive power which they can generate in the beholder who may take myth as actuality.

Ritual

As we have already discussed, symbols may be used for persuasive reasons, but it is not only through symbols, in the sense of them being artefacts, that we can observe symbolic effects, we can consider certain aspects of human behaviour as a manifestation of symbolism. Rituals are symbolic forms of behaviour, and they are often carried out with the intention of creating or sustaining specific forms of behaviour, i.e. they are intended to influence. Symbolic behaviour can be seen as a form of social cohesion, and it was seen in this way by Durkheim (reported in Duncan, 1969, p.158) who said:

> Social sentiments depend on symbols, indeed are
> symbols, because it is only through symbols that
> society becomes conscious of itself and is able
> to ensure the continuation of this consciousness.
> Religious symbols are but one form of this. Coll-
> ective sentiments can become incarnate in persons
> or formulas, and indeed in many kinds of figur-
> ative representations. Symbols, put into conc-
> rete form, evoke strong feelings of identific-
> ation because they are a way of indicating to
> others and ourselves that we participate in a
> common social life. In primitive society the
> clan cannot exist without an emblem or symbol.

In more contemporary terms, we can see examples
of similar uses of symbolic activities for the purpose of evoking feelings of identification, we need
turn no further than to the many political demon-
strations which utilise fully the symbolic importance
of collectivity. It is a ritual activity which high-
lights the relatedness of the participants, thus
evoking some form of satisfaction from an experience
shared, but shared in conformity to a particular set
of rules, rules often hallowed by tradition and thus
sustaining some mythological import. And, as Edelman
(1977) pointed out, participation in the actual business of politics, as distinct from ritual participation, is a minority activity, for the majority it
is more of a symbolic activity. Of course, this is
not to imply that the symbolic involvement of the
majority may not have practical consequences, it
clearly does in terms of votes cast. But it does
imply that for the majority it is more of a ritual
form of behaviour.

Media and symbolisation

Contemporary life is symbolised to a large degree by
the way it is represented in the mass media; because
the source is at a 'distance' from the readership,
a state of omnipotence is created, things are blurred.
Here we can detect a similarity with mythological
processes; time collapses, events crowd into one,
the individual is engaged but at the same time remote,
drama is heightened but realistic detail is minimal;
in other words, the 'form' is more substantial than
the 'meaning', but, unsuspectingly it can appear to
be the meaning, not as proxy, but in reality. So
we can see the connection with myth and metalanguage,
a language which talks about itself, celebrating form
rather than meaning. Witness the use of television

as a persuasive device in political party broadcasts.
What we are generally offered is an image, a one-sided
image with no internal contradictions or possibility
of negative interpretations; controversy, if it exists
relates only to the existence of opposing parties, who
are invariably shown in a negative light, a kind of
darkness to be avoided. We are offered an idealised
future; because the future can only be grasped sym-
bolically it always lends itself to idealisation.
Thus we can see how promises can be endlessly deferred
when they are couched in an ideal, set in the future.
This is similar to the point made by Berger (1972)
about contemporary advertising; the idea that advertising is a deferment of gratification, that it talks
always in the future tense. Of course it would be
rather surprising to see an advertisement which was
concerned with the past, except when it calls upon
the past as a base for the future.

Whether we discuss the influence of symbols in
terms of media or in terms of rituals, we are inevitably drawn back to the importance of codes, and
here we include codes in the widest sense, including
language-objects and ritualised processes. Codes
make possible a metalanguage which can turn upon itself, talk can take the place of action, and it can
be recycled endlessly. The material for this is the
symbol; man is the sculptor who both fashions the
symbol, and then observes life through it. Symbolic
man works in abstracts, and in abstracts all things
are possible. Symbols take on representative values,
and it is the representative values as portrayed in
the media that we turn our attention towards in the
next chapter.

SUMMARY

1. Symbols and symbolic behaviour can both be employ-
    ed in the act of persuasion. Being metaphors,
    they can 'stand in' for other intentions.

2. The persuasive power of symbols resides in their
    ability to evoke associations, such associations
    may appear natural when, in fact, they are his-
    torically determined.

3. Myth plays on the analogy between meaning and
    form; form can become meaning, and meaning can
    become form.

4. The naturalisation of arbitrary symbolic relat-
    ionships allows scope for deception which may
    possess persuasive overtones.

5. One of the functions of ritualistic, symbolic behaviour is the stabilisation of conventions; thus its persuasive import is towards maintenance of the status quo.

6. Symbols, as source material, can be condensed and recoded, thus offering opportunities for the 'borrowing' of ready-made images which can be placed in new contexts.

REFERENCES

BAGGALEY, J. and DUCK, S. (1976) Dynamics of Television, Farnborough, Hants.: Saxon House.

BARTHES, R. (1973) Mythologies. St. Albans: Paladin.

BERGER, J. (1972) Ways of Seeing. Harmondsworth: Penguin.

DUNCAN, H.D. (1969) Symbols and Social Theory. New York: Oxford University Press.

EDELMAN, M. (1977) The Symbolic Uses of Politics Urbana, Ill.: University of Illinois Press.

FIRTH, R. (1973) Symbols: public and private. London: Allen & Unwin.

GOMBRICH, E.H. (1962) Art and Illusion. London: Phaidon.

JUNG, C.G. (1964) Man and His Symbols. London: Aldus Books.

LEACH, E. (1976) Culture and Communication. Cambridge: Cambridge University Press.

SAXL, F. (1970) A Heritage of Images. Harmondsworth: Penguin.

WILDEN, A. (1977) System and Structure. London: Tavistock.

Chapter Ten

MEDIA MANIPULATION

In the last chapter we were concerned to discover the
part that symbolism plays in persuasion, and we noticed particularly the way in which form and meaning
can become interchangeable in the mind of the individual, thus producing a state of awareness which sustains mythology. Form, as we well know, is not only
present in myths, it is the essence of all communication, without form there exists only randomness, and
randomness is the polarity of information. The giving
of form is central to the act of communication, therefore we need to turn our attention to the effects
that differences in form can create.

Seen from a cultural perspective, freed from
emotionally 'loaded' connotations, the study of form
can be very satisfying. For example, one can study
the form created by the artist when he applies paint
to canvas; likewise, one can study the form or arr-
angement of words made by the poet. But when the
issue under scrutiny is that of persuasion, rather
than culture, the concept of manipulation is invoked.
In practical terms, whether the issue is culture or
persuasion, it is a fact that all media has to be
manipulated, but the term manipulation resonates with
physical handling, and shaping by omnipotent beings
for pliant recipients. However, given that media
has to be shaped or given form, irrespective of any
ethical considerations, we need to be aware of the
actual mechanics of media manipulation, although we
must be reminded that the form of the signifier in
communication can never by wholly detached from the
ideology which motivates the content.

Giving of form
The shaping and giving of form to the media of communication is a part of man's cultural heritage. In
pictorial terms, we find that the history of art is

replete with examples of the ways in which images
have been fabricated to produce particular responses
in the minds of the viewers. The techniques and
materials of the visual arts are ideal for the creation of perceptual illusions, so much so that Gombrich
(1960) could devote a lengthy treatise to uncovering
their historical antecedents. Works of art are not
mirrors, as Gombrich said, but they contain the elus-
ive essence of transformation. Here we are on similar ground to mythology, transformation as a kind of
magic; but the magic lies in the perceptual illusions
to which individuals are prone, and the ways in which
images are constructed for the purpose of generating
illusions. The most obvious example is the use of
perspective, which creates the illusion of a three-
dimensional image on a two-dimensional space.

The transformations required in the creation of
mental illusions rest upon man's semiotic potential,
the ability to give signification without concrete
verification. This same condition opens up an infinite variety of possibilities for deception, particularly at the first stage of perceptual registration.
Man, as a reflective, conscious being, also has the
potential to rationalise his perceptions, but below
his conscious awareness there exist cues or pointers
which can orient him towards a particular interpretation rather than another. And it is through these
'below awareness' cues that media can be manipulated
for the purpose of exerting covert influences. On
the other hand, cues might be quite explicit, leaving
the reader/viewer in no doubt as to the intention
behind the message; it would be misleading to impute
covert intentions to all persuasive messages, many
are quite explicit in declaring their purpose.

The work of Barthes (1968) provides some useful
ideas for the consideration of the form of messages.
The form of the message, in his terminology, is the
rhetoric; here we must accept a definition of rhetoric,
not as an emotively charged word, but as a technical
definition describing the articulatory structure of
messages. This definition accords with the earlier
statement in this chapter that media has to be shaped
or given form, irrespective of any ethical considerations. It is here, of course, that aesthetics has
its raison d'être, a pure consideration of form for
form's sake. But, to return to Barthes, although he
made a clear distinction between form (rhetoric) and
content, he, nevertheless, was quite explicit in
pointing out that the form of a message can affect
its interpretation; there is, so to speak, an infiltration of content by form, as though the signifier

and signified had a natural rather than an arbitrary
bond. And here we return to the origins of mythological thought which we discussed earlier.

The interplay between signifier and signified,
i.e. between the form and content, is just one element in the intertwining of the totality of a message; there is another element and that is between
the person and the medium. As was previously stated,
working through any medium imposes some element of
manipulation, and this manifests itself as style.
The style can be that of a particular school (in art)
or convention, and it will inevitably include the
style, or the 'finger print' of the individual communicator (whatever the material he might be using),
thus it happens that a work of art possesses unique-
ness through this very fact of personal identity,
which is difficult to fake, at least to the experienced eye.

The use of any particular medium of expression
imposes an immediate constraint upon the wielder of
that medium, it also carries with it certain potentialities. Therefore, when the potentialities are
known they can be exploited for the purpose of creating particular desired effects, an example is film
editing which makes possible the re-arrangement of
temporal sequences, thus presenting a false impression of time. However, when there is no intention to
create false impressions, a paradox exists that however much man desires to free his message from the
influence of the form or rhetoric, the medium itself
makes demands which can be influential in their own
right. Even in the most direct and immediate forms
of communication, namely speech, there exists the
underlying persuasive potential of the paralinguistic
and prosodic elements, for example, voice modulation
and tone. In personal, face-to-face encounters, small
micro-clues generally surround the delivery of a message, thus giving the receiver some indication of the
sender's covert feelings which he, the sender, may
desire to hide. In contrast, media are more opaque,
they lend themselves to more concealed treatments,
and being delivered separately from their source,
they bear no physical attachment to the originator,
except of course in those media where instant transmission is possible, e.g. live television, but even
here some contrivance is possible.

It is only on reflection, and reflection aided
by specific knowledge of techniques of production,
that we may fully recognise the manipulative or exploitive aspects of media. Psychologically speaking,
ke in the whole or the 'gestalt' before we

discover the constituent parts. At the moment of
apprehension the content may be more compelling than
the rhetoric or form, which may be disguised in order
to hide the underlying intentions of the message.
For example, at the level of below conscious awareness, the structure of the message can be such that
the receiver is guided by cues towards certain interpretations, towards a pre-planned destination, to use
a spatial metaphor. It is, so to speak, at hidden
junctions that the message originator can implant
his route markers. In providing markers, connotation
is reduced, and thus the message originator, be he
film maker or television producer, can guide or manipulate the receiver towards an interpretation of
his own choosing. This is a kind of cueing process
which may take the form of heightening attention to
a particular feature, to the presentation of symbolic
features, or to the juxtaposition of certain items
bearing emotive potential, and, of course, there are
other techniques which we will discuss later.

However, the use of cueing devices can only be
successful when the receiver possesses the necessary
repertoire for interpretation. Once again, we can
invoke the work of MacKay (1969) to explain the underlying process; the sender or communicator has to
choose from the receiver's repertoire or conditional
state of mental readiness for meaning to be 'received'
in the way in which it is 'intended'. Of course, the
cues may not be understood overtly by the receiver,
they may have been established through the conventions
of society, but they do, nevertheless, guide interpretation in some specific way. The wider the message
impact, the more it must conform to cues which are
understood by the population in general, and in this
respect we can note the use of common stereotypes
to guide interpretation, for example, the sartorial
use of black to mark the sinister character in western films.

Cueing devices

The use of markers or cues to effect particular or
required denotations and connotations is not without
interpretative problems, as can be seen from the variety of interpretations that different people give
to the same stimulus or presented message. The less
restricted or stereotyped is the mode of presentation,
the greater the potential for differences in interpretation. It is possible for a single signifier to
'set in motion' a number of alternative routes of
interpretation. Even within one individual, interpretation can 'run off' in a number of directions; with

x number of individuals the possibilities for proliferation of meaning are increased pro rata.   In
order to avoid such proliferation of interpretations,
markers can be inserted which cue the receiver into
intended or desired modes of interpretation.   These
markers can be likened to cues which guide people in
skilled performances; wherever ambiguity exists a
cue can be inserted to simplify choice to a designated
pathway.   This can be considered as manipulative or
in our terms persuasive when it achieves the sender's
objective.   Cues can be in the form of images, shapes
or colours, or they can be linguistic, guiding the
reader to certain desired interpretations, in a way
similar to verbal road signs.

    Our concern here has been to emphasise the man-
ipulative aspects of media presentation, to direct
attention to the form rather than the content which
is more of an ideological issue, and one we shall
touch upon in a later chapter.   We have focused attention on the rhetoric, while at the same time being
aware that the ideology that motivates any particular
message helps to determine its signifiers.   Now we
turn towards an analysis of the various techniques
that are employed in the 'mass' media: namely, print,
especially newspapers and journals; cinema; and television.   In McLuhan's (1962) terms, the first in the
list belongs to the mechanical age, and the other two
belong to the electrical age.   However, because the
press can carry photographic images, all three media
share a common characteristic in being able to convey
information in the form of the analogue.   A crucial
difference is that both film and television deal with
movement, whereas images in the press are static;
nevertheless, although they are static, there is a
kind of interaction or 'spreading effect' from image
to type and from type to image.

Press

The press, as indeed all media, can be analysed for
content, for ownership, for editorial policy, for
distribution, and for readership, which can be sub-
divided into a number of social categories.   But our
concern here is with its physical form, which could,
of course, be dictated by any of the preceding factors.
The press, in its beginnings, was essentially a verbal
means of communication, designed to be read linearly.
However, with the introduction and growth of mass
circulation newspapers, there has been an increasing
tendency towards the inclusion of pictorial illustrations.   During the same period there have also been
changes in typographical formats; headlines in large

type have become more common, even when the events
to be reported are trivial. This shift towards ease
of apprehension and minimal demands on linear pro-
gression, emphasises the change towards mass circulation, to the idea of a readership which prefers
immediacy and ease of apprehension. The apparent
immediacy of pictorial illustrations, here the word
immediacy is used in its original sense as meaning
not mediated, opens avenues for concealed manipulation.
As previously mentioned, in relation to the work of
Barthes (1977), the pictorial image lends itself
ideally to deception; it can be subjected to, for
example, trick photography, retouching and montage.
Through such techniques the finished or published
product can undergo extensive revisions, but what it
still retains is its form as analogue, and thus, to
use the language of Barthes, it retains its 'birth-
right', as an apparent message without a code, it is
only 'apparent' because with increasing familiarity
iconic (analogical) representations themselves become
conventional.
      The pictorial image possesses other character-
istics, it can quicken the reading of the associated
text, it can also lead the reader into that text, in
preference to other text on the same page. And, as
it is an image, it can more readily be retained in
memory than a corresponding verbal description. Also,
pictures provide visual relief when placed in a page
containing a heavy mass of type; even so called
serious newspapers break most of their pages with
scattered pictures, scattered in a proportional rather
than a random way. The greater the circulation of
the newspaper, the greater is the tendency towards
pictorial illustration. For people unaccustomed to
serious reading this kind of presentation has obvious
advantages, but it can reinforce editorial preference
for news of pictorial interest, or if not news, then
items of visual interest. But irrespective of content
interest, the desire for relief from the visual bore-
dom of lines of type is shown by the occasional insertion of lines, known by printers as rules, in the
columns of type. This, of course, is not an issue
for persuasion, but it does demonstrate a control or
manipulation intended to produce specific effects on
the readership.
      Another factor which we need to consider is that
of position; the attention given to any particular
item of news or advertisement can be a product of the
actual position in which it is placed. This is reflected in the difference in advertising rates comm-
anded on the strength of position only, for example,

space near the main editorial tends to be more expensive than space in less prestigious positions. In
this connection it is worth mentioning that there
exists also the possibility of 'cross fertilisation'
from editorial to advertisement; this can happen
when the editorial is concerned with the theme or
intention of the advertisement. It is not uncommon,
particularly in the local press, for collusion to
take place between those responsible for the news
content and those responsible for filling the advertising space to ensure that the editorial gives support to the advertisement. Another device or technique
is the use of contrast effects, a space left predominantly white (while those around are solid in type
or illustration) is thrown into relief and thus becomes more commanding. Of course the reverse is also
possible, in a predominantly white area a solid mass
can gain attention. These are devices for gaining
attention, there are many others, such as the use of
colour, which emphasises the importance of contrast.

Film
Film presents a variety of techniques which can be
exploited for the purpose of creating specific responses in the viewer. In an artistic or creative
sense such exploitation could be looked upon with
favour, that is, when the intention is known to be
motivated not for commercial gain or propagandist
aims, but for the personal satisfaction of the viewer.
Film possesses all those characteristics that we discussed in relation to the photograph, but it possesses,
in addition, the illusory power to suggest movement.
Movement can be speeded up or slowed down, thus there
exists a kind of magic element, and this puts us again
on similar territory to mythology. That which is
merely semiotic can appear real, at least in a tran-
sitory way, emotion can be heightened, time and distance can be collapsed into a present, into a 'here
and now'.
    Through the controlled use of lighting, focusing,
editing and montage, covert influences can be exerted
on the interpretation of the film. Symbolic representations can be made, thus drawing on their power
to act as metaphors possessing strong emotional charge.
The stock of symbols in society provides a ready-made
fund of images which the film-maker can use in the
creation of his message or story. As mentioned earlier, many such images or symbols are stereotypes, but
this is not to decry their usefulness as a means for
conveying ideas or emotions.
    The persuasive power of film, that is the ability

for it to create an illusion of reality and to bring
forth emotive responses in an audience is well attes-
ted, we hardly need any experimental evidence to
prove the point. Until television replaced the cinema as a major form of entertainment, cinema atten-
dances themselves provided sufficient evidence of the
drawing power of film as a medium for providing emotional experience. But it is a contrived medium, as
is all media; it can be subjected to a number of manipulative processes. For example, shots have to be
selected, and the whole edited into a continuous
sequence, which may initially be in fragmentary parts.
To the extent that film-making is a task involving
a wide number of selections, for example, location,
time, lighting, it must inevitably produce bias, the
bias of the producer; it can be likened to the way
in which man filters his sensory experiences to
fit in with a pre-established framework of interpretation. The film producer shapes and orders his product to fit in with an idea, or framework, to give
a specific form, but the materials and techniques at
hand make their own demands on the form which is
achieved. It is a symbiotic process.
    The actual success achieved by the producer is
dependent upon the audience sharing some of his knowledge and the codes and conventions which he uses,
thus enabling them to identify the symbolic significance of the information which is presented. In terms
of persuasive influence, part of the task of the film-
maker is the juxtaposition of images, but only of
images shared in the audience's reference system. It
is possible, of course, to establish within a film
certain denoted references, in fact part of the job
of any narrative, whether it be presented in the form
of a film or book, is to identify or characterise by
denotation, which then can carry subsequent connotative
potential.
    Whatever the aim of the producer, the task before
him is one of setting-up particular relationships;
relationships between events, relationships between
images, relationships between sound and vision, relationships between what is on the screen and the resources that the audience has for interpreting what is
presented. In creating these relationships, the producer has to manipulate the material of film, to in-
vent through the potentialities of the medium. When
he directs attention to the material in its own right,
when he exploits the inner tensions within the material itself the intention is aesthetic, however, when
the intention is to produce effects not related to
the material per se, but to some other objective,

then a persuasive intention can be ascribed. But whatever the intention the underlying fact is that form has to be given to the medium, it has to be manipulated.

Television

Television shares many of the same properties as film, and it is open to similar forms of manipulation, although it does carry a greater potential of immediacy. Pictures can be transmitted at the actual time of events thus adding to the sense of participation. However, there is one crucial difference between cinematic viewing and television viewing, and that is the relationship to others. In the cinema the darkness tends to isolate the viewer, and, except in the case of humorous films, the presence of others tends not to influence personal response. In contrast, television is usually viewed in non-darkened conditions, where the presence of others is felt more acutely. This awareness of the presence of others and of their reactions adds another dimension to the way in which the medium influences the viewer. From the work of Kelley and Woodruff (1956) on the influence of the group, we can discern how the composition of an audience can create a tendency towards shared beliefs. They found that messages received greater endorsement when it was known that other members of the group held similar views. In an attempt to discover whether the showing of audience reaction to a televised programme would have a similar effect, Baggaley and Duck (1976) presented two groups of subjects with a televised lecture on a topic which was unfamiliar to them. One group was shown the televised lecture with inserted positive audience reactions; the other group was shown the same lecture, but this time the inserted information showed negative audience reactions. The outcome was that the group who had been shown the tape with the negative audience responses considered that the lecturer on the tape was less expert than the group who had been shown the tape with the favourable audience responses, despite the fact that the only difference in presentation was the type of audience response which was edited into the lecture sequence. The authors concluded their observation of the results by declaring that (p.95)'these results indicate the immense illusory power of the editing process generally and the clear propagandist uses to which it can be put.'

In addition to studying the effect of the reactions of audiences by inserted items, the work of Baggaley and Duck has other interesting implications

for our theme of persuasion. For example, they
looked at the effect of other manipulative strategies
or presentational variables:

    (i)   variation of camera angle;

    (ii)   addition of visual background to the
            performer or presenter;

   (iii)   variation of facial direction of the
            presenter, front facing and in profile;

    (iv)   reaction to an interviewer.

In all of these conditions significant effects
were found which led the authors to conclude that the
simple visual imagery of a television production may
actually dominate its verbal content. They summed up
their research findings as follows (p.105):

> The finding, recurrent throughout these exper-
> iments, that presentation techniques may be
> used in order to heighten not only the interest
> value of a production, but also the evident
> credibility and expertise of the programme
> presenter indicates that the effects of presen-
> tation are not only stronger than previously
> supposed, but also more varied. The use of
> television according to the criterion of visual
> interest alone evidently exploits only one of
> its dynamic properties.

This then is a clear demonstration of the potentiality of the medium to produce specific effects,
effects that can be viewed for their persuasive potential, to influence people in a direction known only
to the maker of the programme or his collaborators.
Again we return to the influence of tacit signs, and
it is not only in television viewing that we can see
their importance, they play an important part in social life in general;thus we can conclude that the
reading of tacit signs in 'real' life and in screened
material both stem from the same interpretative framework. That being so, we can refer to work from the
social field in support of our interest in the medium
of television. A useful reference is the work of
Garfinkel (1973, p.22); in discussing the implications
of tacit signs as 'background expectancies' he wrote:

> In accounting for the stable features of every-
> day activities, sociologists commonly select
> familiar settings such as family households or
> work places and ask for the variables that con-

tribute to their stable features. Just as commonly one set of considerations are unexamined; the socially standardised and standardising, 'seen but unnoticed', expected background features of everyday scenes. The member of the society uses background expectancies as a scheme of interpretation... Demonstrably he is responsive to this background, while at the same time he is at a loss to tell us specifically of what the expectancies consist.

So, as in real life, the television viewer is also subject to expectancies which guide him towards specific interpretations, and these expectancies find their support in tacit signs, and being tacit, they are below conscious awareness. Hence when the intention of a programme is to influence the viewer in a particular way by the use of tacit signs, the producer must know the stock of signs from which he can draw. Once known, these signs can then be inserted into the context of a programme as background material, which guides or gives signification to the foreground or explicit material. Of course, when the viewer is alerted to these possibilities, he has at his disposal a means of decoding the structure. A general awareness of the codes and conventions used in media production is one way of resisting their persuasive influences.

The intention to influence or persuade others through the use of visual images requires a knowledge of various techniques for it to be given effect. When the intention is proclaimed, as in most advertisements, the viewer can accept the offered images for what they are on the screen, as a form of metacommunication, and known as such. On the other hand, when their intentions are not overtly disclosed, they can be a potent source of covert influence as the work of Baggaley (1980) and Baggaley and Duck (1976) demonstrated.

The framing of images for television, cinema or photographs in the press, puts a three-dimensional world into a two-dimensional context. However, man exists in a three-dimensional world, he also lives in direct communication with others without the intervention of mediated devices. What are the persuasive influences of belonging to groups? To this question, we now turn out attention.

SUMMARY

1. All media are subject to manipulation, that is they have to be given form.

2. The giving of form to any means of expression is its rhetoric.

3. Moving images can give the illusion of the collapsing of space and time, thus, the 'then and there' can become the 'here and now'.

4. Cues can be inserted to guide the reader/viewer to intended interpretations, such cues may be overt or covert.

5. The known responses of others can affect individual responses.

6. Editing can be influential in determining the credibility of a televised presenter, so also can specific techniques of production.

REFERENCES

BAGGALEY, J. (1980) Psychology of the TV Image.
    Farnborough, Hants: Gower Publishing Co.
BAGGALEY, J. and DUCK, S. (1976) Dynamics of Television. Farnborough, Hants: Saxon House.
BARTHES, R. (1968) Elements of Semiology. New York:
    Hill & Wang.
BARTHES, R. (1977) Image, Music, Text. London:
    Fontana.
ECO, U. (1977) A Theory of Semiotics. London:
    Macmillan.
GARFINKEL, H. (1973) Background expectancies. In
    Douglas, M. (ed.) Rules and Meanings. Harmondsworth: Penguin, pp. 21-23.
GOMBRICH, E.H. (1960) Art and Illusion. London:
    Phaidon Press.
KELLEY, H.H. and WOODRUFF, C.L. (1956) Members
    reactions to apparent group approval of a
    counter-norm communication, Vol. 52, Journal of
    Abnormal Social Psychology.
MacKAY, D.M. (1969) Information, Mechanism and
    Meaning. Cambridge, Mass.: The M.I.T. Press.
McLUHAN, M. (1962) The Gutenberg Galaxy. London:
    Routledge and Kegan Paul.

Chapter Eleven

GROUP INFLUENCES

We have threaded our way through a number of factors
which, in one way or another, have a bearing on persuasion. We have looked through the lens of the
psychologist for individual characteristics; we have
borrowed ideas from semiology in order to analyse the
effect of codes and conventions; and we have seen how
media can be manipulated for the purpose of causing
specific interpretations. However, apart from mentioning ritual activities when we were discussing
symbolism, we have not considered the persuasive effects of groups per se. It is not only in rituals
that we find pressure being exerted towards conformity in beliefs and behaviour, we can observe similar
pressures in non-ritualistic group situations. And
it is towards a consideration of groups as influential or persuasive agencies in their own right that
we now turn our attention.

As individuals we do not exist in isolation
from others, except in rare and unusual circumstances;
the existence of others provides references by which
we can come to know ourselves (Sartre, 1966). Our
beliefs, values and actions are inextricably inter-
woven with other people; they provide a kind of mirror for self-awareness. However, there is a price
to be paid, and this price is the tie or bond which
when formed between self and other, between an individual and a group, can create demands of a particular
kind, demands towards conformity of thought and behaviour appropriate to the situation. Moreover, people
can identify with particular groups to which they do
not belong, known as reference groups, and this identification can lead towards subtle changes in beliefs,
attitudes and actions. Experimental evidence provided
by Siegel and Siegel (1966) shows the influence of
reference groups on attitude change.

Historically the power of group influence has

long been recognised, at least in practical ways;
for example, the army has always been aware of the
value of group loyalty which finds expression in loyalty to other members of a platoon, the army's small-
est operational unit. Although appeals are often
made to some remoter figures, such as the state or
its head, as grounds for loyalty, it is the platoon
or group which creates the most potent force for the
actual display of loyalty, not the abstractions which
are presented as models. In a similar but less dramatic way, we can observe group influences in more
everyday situations. In work groups, in friendship
groups, and other interest groups, the individual is
subjected to influences which can cause him to behave
in a particular way or to hold particular beliefs.
The cohesion of the group demands that its members
forego some of their personal aspirations or desires
when these are likely to be in conflict with group
norms, thus an individual in joining a voluntary group
has a 'trade-off' decision to make, unless of course
he joins with the intention of modifying its ethos.
      In terms of our interest in the act of persuasion,
we can study the influence of groups as persuasive
agencies in two distinct and unique ways. Firstly,
we can direct our attention to the ways in which the
groups acts to influence its constituent members, this
we shall call its internal influence; and secondly,
we can draw attention to its external influence, that
is the influence or pressure that it can exert upon
larger institutions or society. Studies in the area
of the first category tend to stem from social psychology, while studies in the second category, the
external influence, tend to be the province of politics or organisational studies.

Internal influence
Group membership can confer benefits upon its members,
at least that is how it will appear to them when they
are in voluntary attendance; the benefits could be
material or they could be social, and they could be
both material and social. Against these possibilities
costs have to be considered, such costs could be constraints upon personal or idiosyncratic behaviour, as
well as any financial costs. However, it would be
reasonable to assume that the benefits of membership
would outweigh the costs, with the particular exception of people joining the group for philanthropic
rather than instrumental reasons. But whatever the
reasons for joining, the influence of the group can
be quite considerable; even in non-voluntary groups,
epitomised by Schein and others (1961) in their studies

of prisoners of war, there exists considerable influence for attitude change.

Groups can facilitate or inhibit change in their
members, thus they wield a persuasive influence. Our
interest lies essentially in an appreciation of the
group as an agency of change; the way that the group
can cause an individual to bring his beliefs into
line with others in the group as a condition of acceptance. We can see a play upon this condition of
need for acceptance in those advertisements which
offer the promise, but only the promise, of social
acceptance; the offer, of course, is conditional upon
the reader/viewer purchasing the advertised commodity
which is presumed to confer the link with the desired
'others'.

The interdependence, whether it be natural or
socially conditioned, that people have for each other,
and the need for identification, provides a strong
motive for affiliation, and through such affiliation
the potential for influence can be made manifest. But
it is not only affiliation that is important, it is
the self-knowledge that others supply in the way that
they reflect or mirror the individual member that is
also important; they supply frames of reference.
Frames of reference provide the means of personal
evaluation, the standard by which the self is pitted.
It is against this background and the need for affiliation that we should observe the influence of the
group. When the group offers 'frames of reference'
which differ from those brought by the individual,
the individual is faced with three alternatives: (i)
acquiescence with the group's framework; (ii) changing the group's framework; or (iii) withdrawal from
the group. Generally the first alternative is the
least problematic, thus it is found that people tend
to conform, and such action has the tendency to reinforce the existing framework.

Social reinforcement

The need for positive social reinforcement from other
members of the group provides a reason for change
when the person possesses beliefs or values which are
contrary to those of the group. But such change can
only be brought about when the individual is aware of
the differences. It means a re-evaluation of the
individual's position within the group's frame of
reference. And it does appear that as individuals
we know ourselves not only by what we do on our own,
but also by what we do in the presence of others. It
is in this latter respect that our identity or sense
of self is achieved through the confirmation provided

by others (Goffman, 1972), and because we need others
to offer such confirmation, we are then committed to
the influences that the group warrants in other directions.
     Social reinforcement and its effects has been a
focus of study for some considerable time; for example,
Allport (1924) showed how feelings can be canalised
into a similar mode when there exists interaction
between members of an audience. And the same tendency
towards conformity was noted by Eisenson and others
(1963); they noted that the beliefs and actions of
'fellow-listeners' tended to influence other listeners
in the audience to avoid extreme behaviour which would
have set them apart, although in terms of subsequent
behaviour we can only surmise as to what the influence would be. However, we do know from the work of
Schein and others (1961) that indoctrination by group
techniques has no lasting effects when newly acquired
behaviour or attitudes are no longer reinforced. In
short, the persuasive potential of group influence
stemming from coercive situations is restricted to a
specific time interval, unless it is maintained by
subsequent reinforcement. This is the kind of effect
which we would expect from our knowledge of learning
theory which maintains that responses that are not
rewarded tend to diminish or fall away altogether.

Group involvement
A number of studies have been carried out into the
dynamics of groups, from which important implications
arise for persuasion as it is manifested in democratic group processes, here persuasion relates to the
acceptance of decisions made by the group as a collective. In a study by Bennett (1955) he found that
allowing people to take part in the decision-making
process of the group, and achieving veritable consensus, was the main determinant of continuing acceptance of the decisions which had been reached.
This finding echoes in some respects Schein's comm-
ents upon the effects of 'thought reform', a euphemism for indoctrination, which he said was ineffect-
ive when principles were merely recited, rather than
acted upon, he was referring to the attempted indoctrination of American prisoners of war. So the implication is that involvement in a practical way is more
substantial than verbal expression as a means of creating acceptance of the aims and purposes of a group.
Although many factors may contribute to the effectiveness of a group decision; consensus, or near consensus is of extreme importance, in such situations
the holding of contrary views puts the individual in

a more isolated position. This is the kind of outcome which we might expect in democratic groups where
membership is voluntary. However in coercive situations, of the kind found in the studies of prisoners
of war (Schein, 1961), the individual is faced with
having to adapt to a situation out of pure necessity,
with no opportunity to modify its form or procedures.
But when a single other person is seen to be resisting influence, then this strengthens the resistance
of a person who desires not to conform. Such identification with another person does depend, however,
upon the personal qualities of the reference person.
For example, when the other person is judged to be
superior in some way, then this acts as a spur to the
individual who makes the judgement. This relates to
the credibility studies of Hovland (1953) who found
that credibility is one of the most important characteristics for message originators or sources to
possess for communications to be persuasive. This
then leads us to the influence of leaders.

Group leaders
A group leader can be the object of reference, indeed
his leadership depends upon the fact that he plays
this role; therefore we should expect that a leader
would be more influential than other members of a
group. Consequently we need to look more carefully
at leadership and the way in which it functions in
the process of influence or persuasion. From the
work of Katz and Lazarsfeld (1955) we can pick-up
some useful clues regarding the flow of information
from the media to people in general. And here we
can find that influence may flow, not directly from
press to public, but that it may be channelled through what Katz and Lazarsfeld described as opinion
leaders who were better educated and more avid readers of books and journals; this is a partial or restricted view, it is quite possible that other factors
are operative, nevertheless these two variables provided useful and informative indices. This flow of
information became known as a 'two-step flow'; step
one from media to opinion leader; step two from
opinion leader to others by word of mouth. Research
into the influence of opinion leaders in contrast to
media influences was well summed up by Klapper (1967,
p.305):

> The bare bones of the concept of personal in-
> fluence lie in the fact that in reference to
> decisions in various areas of attitude behav-
> iour, people have been found to be influenced

by specific other individuals as strongly or
more strongly than they have been influenced
by mass communication. These others have var-
iously been called opinion leaders, gatekeepers,
influentials, initiators, and taste-makers.
They are not, however, characteristically political leaders or teachers or preachers or
elites. What are the chief characteristics of
opinion leaders? Interestingly enough, they
cannot be characterized as a whole, apart from
those who heed their words. Their chief characteristic is that they can influence the attitudes and opinions of a few people like themselves, typically from one to five others. Even
within that sphere, their leadership seldom
extends beyond a limited range of topics. For
example, the opinion leader heeded on political
matters is likely to carry little weight in
reference to ladies' fashions or the arts. The
influence of the opinion leader is typically
exerted in informal face-to-face discourse and
may or may not be purposive. To date, this
process of personal influence has been studied
in reference to voting; to views on public
issues; everyday fashion and marketing decisions
(etc.)..... In virtually all of these spheres,
the exercise of opinion leadership, or of personal influence, has been found to be as critical or more critical than the influence of
mass communications.

These observations of Klapper emphasise the
specifics of leadership, demonstrating that leadership is not just an issue of personality, but is
related to special knowledge which is used in the
exercise of leadership; of course personality factors
may contribute towards effective leadership, but such
factors are secondary to those of perceived expertise. We cannot let the two-step model of 'information flow' pass without qualification. In work carried out by Menzel and Katz (1955) into the introduction of new drugs into the medical profession, they
found that the simple two-step model was inadequate
to explain the uptake of new drugs by doctors. They
found that the willingness to adopt new drugs bore
a relationship to familiarity with recent professional articles and with attendance at professional
conferences. Doctors who were subjected to these
influences served as reference groups for other coll-
eagues who were professionally less well informed.
The more geographically isolated doctors tended, as

one would expect, to rely on commercial persuasion,
for example direct mail advertisements. But where
the flow of information was carried out through personal contacts it was found that, on occasions, it
would take three or four steps, and not the mere two-
steps mentioned in the work of Katz and Lazarsfeld.
It is not only in the medical profession that such
a process is observable, command structures in many
different fields employ a multi-step flow of communication where information is despatched by interpersonal connections, colloquially known as 'down
the line'.

    We have noted the way in which group membership
has an influential effect upon its members. In particular we have noted that decisions which are reached
through general participation, and bearing a high
degree of unanimity tend to exert strong persuasive
influence. This influence or power rests upon the
establishment of group consensus, group conformity,
and group goals, and because it resides in the group
as a collective rather than in the individual it
bears a special place in the study of persuasion. It
is here also that we must reflect on the limited persuasive power of the mass media and the greater influence of opinion leaders as catalysts, through whom
ideas flow, and in doing so change the medium of presentation from artefactual media to that of verbal
face-to-face communication. There exists also the
ever present possibility of idiosyncratic interpretations on the part of the opinion leader changing
in fundamental ways the ideas or information in the
media. However, with the greater potential for
direct communication made possible by television and
other broadcast media the results could differ. In
this kind of situation there are fewer intermediaries,
but the influence of others is still brought to bear,
the standards they set are used as yardsticks for
judgement even when the 'others' are absent. So what
we need to know in relation to broadcast media is to
what extent direct appeals modify beliefs or attitudes
without reference to third parties. One would suspect, from knowledge gained about the influence of
reference groups, that absent 'others' would help to
determine the way in which behaviour is modified, or
not modified as the case may be; the framework for
interpretation is not limited to the self only, but
reaches out to include significant others.

    What we have emphasised is the power of the
group to cause the individual to act in a particular
way; to inculcate attitudes or beliefs of a particular kind; to cause people to think or act in ways

which they would not necessarily do if they were outside its influence. We have also seen how influence spreads from, and through, people who have established themselves as being authoritative on some topic or other, and that it is communication established at the face-to-face level which tends to carry more weight than does that of the press. All these influences are directed towards individuals; toward individual thought, feelings or behaviour, towards how any one person is modified by virtue of group membership. But there is another direction of influence, and that is from the group as a collective towards other external agencies or institutions.

External influence

We have seen that the mobilisation of consensus within a group provides cohesion for its future action, that the unity so formed is at the expense of the expression of personal desires should they conflict with those of the group. This unity can be turned towards other purposes, it can be used not only for internal influences but it can be turned outwards. This is its other dynamic, the dynamic of being able to exercise its collective power to gain benefits or concessions for its members. For many individuals the reason for joining or belonging to a particular group and remaining faithful to its aims and purposes rests on the assumption that they will derive some personal benefit, a benefit which they could not achieve in isolation from the group. In voluntary groups there exists a cost-benefit decision to be made; whatever the presumed benefit, the cost is always one of some restriction on personal behaviour, but this price is generally acceptable when the gains weigh more heavily than the costs.

The persuasive power of the group in its collectivity is invariably greater than that of any one of its individual members, and this provides one of the most important reasons for joining, despite the ensuing restrictions that this can create in terms of personal freedom, namely the suppression of personal beliefs or feelings when they are in conflict with those derived from group consensus or conformity.

The power or influence stemming from groups penetrates our lives in many ways, in fact it could be argued that the basis of Western democratic societies rests more upon this particular form of power than the ballot box. And in fact, this was a conclusion arrived at by Mills (1956) in his analysis of the power bases of American society. There is little doubt that 'open societies', here the term

open societies is used in the sense employed by
Popper (1962) to describe societies which reject
totalitarianism, lend themselves to group influences,
and that such influences play a vital part in moulding decisions at different levels of society. But
as Castles (1976) pointed out, the ability of groups
and organisations to exert influence on others is
determined by the extent to which they can mobilise
the support of members, and keep them faithful to
group objectives or purposes.

Groups may owe their origin to a deliberate
attempt to create pressure, or they may coincidentally
acquire the ability to exert pressure. For example,
some pressure groups can be found to have an evolut-
ionary history which, in the first instance, was not
oriented towards external influence. Professional
associations provide useful examples of this accret-
ion of power; members join, in the first instance,
for professional reasons, but later the power of the
collective can be turned outside itself, influencing
decisions at other levels of society. This dual role
or dual influence can cause problems for individual
members, particularly when political issues are involved. In such instances tension may arise when
the individual is expected to conform on issues which
he believes are outside the legitimate scope of the
group, but when a person's livelihood depends on
membership of the group, then he is coerced into
acceptance, assuming that he desires to retain membership.

Trade Unions have generated the greatest amount
of notoriety as pressure groups, but as Olson (1976)
pointed out, farm organisations are expected to strive for favourable legislation for their members;
cartels are expected to strive for higher prices for
participating firms; corporations are expected to
further the interests of their stockholders; and the
state is expected to further the common interests of
its citizens. In many instances the power potential
of the corporate body may be inadequate to achieve
the aims or objecives of its constituent members as
expressed in group terms, in which case lobbying
programmes may be devised. And it is in this area
of lobbying that we can notice a marked growth of
activity, so much so, that it has now become a professional activity in its own right. Lobbyists have
become paid intermediaries, mediating between clients
and parliament, similar in a way to advertising agents
mediating between clients and media producers.

The employment of lobbyists, of public relations
consultants, and of advertising agents, exemplifies

the use of formal agencies, which themselves have their raison d'être in putting forward particular points of view with the intention of influencing decisions, beliefs or values. It is a legalised form of pleading carried out at many different levels of society, and it is usually carried out for the benefit of particular groups which could be political, social or economic, or indeed others unspecified.

In this chapter we have dealt with group influences under two categories or headings; firstly we dealt with the internal effects on constituent members; and secondly we looked at the external influences. Whether we focus on the internal or external influences, power resides in the existence of the group as a collective, superseding any one individual, but nevertheless, requiring individuals to make some voluntary choices in the light of 'trade-off' values. This of course refers more particularly to voluntary groups; in coercive situations the 'trade-off' values are somewhat different. We have also considered the influence, or the lack of influence, of the mass media. Compared with face-to-face communication, mediated communication appears to be less influential, but face-to-face communication is not always persuasive, it depends upon a number of factors, the most important being the credibility of the message carrier. Our interest in groups as agencies for persuading or influencing others has led us into the wider territory of society, we have ventured onto the ground of lobbying, now we must view other aspects, particularly advertising, propaganda, and ideology, for the contribution which studies in these areas can make to the general theme of persuasion.

SUMMARY

1. Groups possess the potential to modify the beliefs, values and aspirations of their individual members, hence they possess persuasive potential.

2. Group membership brings constraints. When membership is voluntary, members are faced with cost-benefit decisions.

3. Interdependence and the need for identification provide strong motives for affiliation, which carries with it a persuasive potential.

4. Group consensus has a strong influence in maintaining conformity to group goals and norms.

5. Group leaders act as catalysts: their persuasive potential rests upon their credibility.

6. Groups possess the potential for internal or
    external influence: internal influence is that
    directed toward 'shaping' their constituent
    members; external influence is that directed
    towards other factions of society.

REFERENCES

ALLPORT, F.H. (1924) Social Psychology. Boston:
    Houghton Mifflin.
BENNETT, E.B. (1955) Discussion, decision, commit-
    ment and consensus in group decision. Human
    Relations, vol. 8, pp.251-273.
CASTLES, F.G. (ed.) (1976) Decisions, Organisations
    and Society. Harmondsworth: Penguin.
EISENSON, J., AUER, J.J. and IRWIN, J.V. (1963) The
    Psychology of Communication. New York:
    Appleton-Century-Crofts.
GOFFMAN, E. (1972) Interaction Ritual. Harmondsworth:
    Penguin.
HOVLAND, C.I., JANIS, I.L. and KELLEY, H.H. (1953)
    Communication and Persuasion. New Haven:
    Yale University Press.
KATZ, E. and LAZARSFELD, P.F. (1955) Personal
    Influence. New York: The Free Press.
KLAPPER, J.T. (1967) Mass communication, attitude
    stability and change. In Sherif, C.W. and
    Sherif, M. (eds.) Attitude, Ego-Involvement and
    Change. New York: John Wiley, pp. 297-309.
MENZEL, H. and KATZ, E. (1955) Social relations and
    innovation in the medical profession: the epid-
    emiology of a new drug. Public Opinion
    Quarterly, vol. 19, pp. 337-352.
MILLS, C.W. (1956) The Power Elite. Oxford: Oxford
    University Press.
OLSON, M. (1976) Groups and organizations and their
    basis of support. In Castles, F.G. et al (eds.)
    Decisions, Organizations and Society.
    Harmondsworth: Penguin, pp. 147-160.
POPPER, K.R. (1962) The Open Society and its Enemies.
    London: Routledge and Kegan Paul.
SARTRE, J.P. (1966) Being and Nothingness. New
    York: Washington Square Press.
SCHEIN, E.H., SCHNEIER, I. and BARKER, C.H. (1961)
    Coercive Persuasion. New York: W.W. Norton & Co.
SIEGEL, A.E. and SIEGEL, S. (1966) Reference groups,
    membership groups, and attitude change. In
    Warren, N. and Jahoda, M. (eds.) Attitudes.
    Harmondsworth: Penguin, pp. 129-138.

Chapter Twelve

SOCIETY AND PERSUASION

We have seen the way that individual or personal
factors bear upon the processes of persuasion, and
in the last chapter we saw how groups provide a particular source of influence. However, apart from mentioning the importance of opinion leaders in the flow
of information, we have not considered the wider
aspects of persuasion as it relates to society in
general. At this level of analysis the focus of attention shifts from face-to-face communication towards
mediated forms of communication and in doing so it
becomes concerned with distance as a factor, i.e.the
separation between sender and receiver. This separation means that an analysis of persuasive effects
needs to take into account other variables which can
militate against or facilitate them.
    Persuasion, whether it is carried out at a dis-
tance or in immediate situations has to contend with
all the various individual factors which we discussed
earlier. And the first consideration is that of attention; without some form of at least minimal attention, persuasive appeals are blunted from the outset.
Even when attention has been gained there is no guar-
antee that any lasting results will be achieved.
When an individual is free to choose his priorities,
priorities of money expenditure, of the investment
of time, etc., persuasive appeals are forced to compete, and in such competition the practicalities of
living will tend to be given preference. And it is
against this background that we can observe advertisements concerned with selling 'non-essentials'
directing their appeals to irrational motives, to
covert desires which are usually suppressed when subjected to rational consideration.
    Despite the emphasis given by some writers to
the negative aspects of persuasion, often carrying
the assumption of compliant recipients, it is possible

to put forward the opposite point of view and to
stress the natural or acquired resistance that people
possess to all forms of persuasive appeals. In situations where there exists some freedom of choice,
it does the average person less than justice to assume
that he is not capable of apportioning his limited
resources in a way most to his liking, this is of
course an ethical point, but it is worth emphasising.
And although people may be given to day-dreaming,
they are generally quite capable of distinguishing
between reality and fiction. It is of course quite
possible that appeals to covert desires may be effective, but such effect needs to be demonstrated rather
than assumed; it would appear to be more accurate to
believe that people are not inherently gullible, that
they are usually able to detect persuasive intention
and fantasy when it is generated through the media.

It could be argued that the amount of money
spent on advertising gives some indication of the
resistance to be overcome. For example, despite the
vast amount of money spent by the British Government
on advertising the dangers of excessive alcohol for
car drivers, and the desirability of wearing seat
belts in cars, no great success was met until legislation was introduced for some form of law enforce-
ment covering these two aspects of car driving.

With the above considerations in mind, we can
go on to discuss persuasion at the societal level
with particular emphasis on advertising and propaganda, the two main forms of organised persuasion.
Very often the terms advertising and propaganda are
used in an interchangeable way; however, a useful
distinction to bear in mind is that advertising is
generally directed towards commercial ends and financial rewards, whereas propaganda has a less restricted meaning, relating more to political or other
ends without commercial motives. We can, however,
find some cross linkage between advertising and propaganda when we invoke the concept of ideology, both
advertising and propaganda take place against a cultural background which can be defined in ideological
terms, and it is towards ideology that our attention
will turn in the latter part of this chapter.

Advertising

The deployment of persuasion for commercial gain is
not an entirely new phenomenon, in a primitive way
it can be seen to have its origins in the selling
of wares in the market-place. However our interest
here lies in the more specialised and professional
uses of advertising, particularly as it is practised

by big-business through its formal agencies. Criticism of advertising generally begins from a negative bias, but it is worth recalling that a large proportion of advertising is informative in its content, for example advertising in the technical press. This point is mentioned not for the purpose of justifying advertising, but to create some form of balance in its assessment. It is often difficult to separate the informative from the persuasive in messages or advertisements; the informative can be persuasive, and conversely, that which is persuasive by intent may also be informative.

Whichever way we view advertising, its motive, or more correctly the motive of its progenitors, is that of persuasion; persuasion to make a particular purchase; to travel by a particular carrier; to think well of a particular branded commodity; to accept the projected image of the advertiser. The target of attention is the consumer, and consumer oriented advertising is inextricably bound to mass production. Mass production has created the need for mass selling, and conversely, mass selling has created the need for mass production. It has become circular with each factor being dependent on the other.

Advertising can be studied from a number of different approaches: the economist is concerned with advertising as part of the marketing equation; the sociologist is concerned with its social implications; the psychologist is interested in the personal factors; while the professional advertising agent is interested in all three provinces. Of the three approaches, it is the psychological one which tends to generate the most heated discussions about the place of advertising in society, particularly when Freudian theorising and ideas from the Behaviourist School are enlisted as explanations. Moreover, we can even go further and notice the way in which concepts emanating from social-anthropology have been borrowed for the purpose of explaining non-rational advertising messages. For example, Gossage (1967) gave an explanation of advertising's ephemeral or non-rational basis in terms of magic as put forward in Sir James Frazer's (1935) book the 'Golden Bough'. For our purposes it is Frazer's concept of practical magic which is of most interest. Practical magic, as conceived by Frazer, implies a form of transformation which is achieved through a body of rules, the following of the rules or ritual makes possible the transformation. But of central concern to our interest is the symbolic aspect of the procedure, the taking possession by symbolic means of that which is absent but associated. This is

not a condition created by advertising, it is a condition of 'symbolic man', but it is used by advertising to suit its own purposes. It is also closely
connected to the concept of imagination, through the
enlistment of imagery and the possibility of psychologically collapsing time and space so that the 'Then
and There' becomes the 'Here and Now'. It is the
basis of mythological thought and, as such, it is a
part of man, of his history, and of the way that he
comes to terms with the apparently inexplicable.
Without the propensity to imagine, to make present
that which is absent, in other words to take possession of something lacking in oneself, advertising as
a persuasive force would hardly exist. This is the
ephemeral aspect of the business.

Psychology, as a discipline, has provided a
number of well researched areas which are relevant
to advertising, for example the work on memory and
motivation. Freudian concepts, with their strong
emphasis on motivation, have been enlisted to explain
apparently irrational buying preferences, and to demonstrate the deep seated motives which make the choices in the first place. Packard (1962) invented the
apt journalistic expression the 'hidden persuaders'
to describe the attempts of advertisers to enlist
motivations of a deep seated or unconscious nature.
However, while Freudian insights provide interesting
ways of explaining sources of motivation at the level
of the unconscious, they are not the only source to
which we can turn in order to explain covert motives.
For example we can find useful ideas for our theme
in the work of Veblen (1970), ideas drawn from social
theory which stress the contrast between latent and
manifest reasons of behaviour. According to Veblen
the manifest reason for the purchase of goods is the
satisfaction gained from the purpose for which the
goods have been designed; for example the manifest
reason for the purchase of a motor car is that it
provides a means of transport. However, the same
purchase could be described at another level, the
latent level. At this level the purchase possesses
symbolic value, it is conspicuous for this reason.
In describing this contrast between the manifest and
the latent reasons for purchasing commodities, Veblen
used the apt term conspicuous consumption to describe
the purchase of commodities for their social or symbolic value. It represents the buying of commodities
as images, images which derive their value from a
social context; they are images serving a status
function in which the buying equation is not between
cost and product excellence, but between cost and

social effect. The vernacular expression for this
behaviour is 'keeping up with the Jones'. Whether a
Freudian or Veblenian perspective is adopted will
depend upon the circumstances or underlying intention
behind the advertisement. To decode advertisements,
one has to have an extensive range of codes at one's
finger tips. It is not always necessary to search
for deep seated motives, many advertisements declare
their purpose quite openly, while others need to be
read at a below surface level for their purpose to
be detected. It always makes for more excitement to
search for ephemeral qualities and to eschew the
many forms of factual advertising which declare themselves purposefully at the manifest level. Berger's
(1972) work is a good example of selective criticism
of advertising; he exposed the negative aspect of
'glamour' as portrayed by the fashion industry. It
could be argued that the selling of images, the term
used to describe the trade of goods for their symbolic
value, reflects genuine desire, that this desire is
in evidence whether advertising exists or not, and
that it is a reflection of a human condition. The
objection could then be raised that it is a human
condition which is exploited for commercial gain.

One of the major weaknesses of the critics of
advertising is that they attempt to analyse or decode
advertisements as images without presenting evidence
of the effects that the images actually produce. It
is at the level of received meaning as defined by
MacKay (1969) that we need to pitch our analysis for
a more critical judgement to be made. It is quite
possible that intended meaning generated overtly or
covertly may have no effect on the receiver. The
first line of defence is the perceptual mechanism
itself; as we saw in our earlier discussion on memory,
the perceptual mechanism is selective, which means
that equal priority is not accorded to all incoming
information. Generally speaking, information which
is peripheral to one's own thoughts or aspirations
stands a far greater chance of being accorded low
priority in attention, and certainly in memory. It
is to overcome this tendency that many advertisements
attempt to provide a kind of realism, a realism which
identifies, or attempts to do so, with the aspirations of the recipient of the communication. But here
again the presentation is mediated, and being mediated it is distinguishable from 'real' life, and thus
it is subject to the censorship of practicality.

Propaganda

The basic concern of advertising is with commercial-
ism, but the phenomenon of propaganda to which we now
turn has different connotations. The term propaganda
has gathered to itself sinister overtones, owing to
its connections with totalitarian systems of government, and yet its origins lie in religious affairs.
The term propaganda was derived from the proceedings
of the Roman Catholic Church, which promulgated a
'Congregatio de Propaganda Fide' in the 17th Century
for the purpose of co-ordinating its missionary activities (Kecskemeti, 1973). The Soviet-Marxist concept of propaganda still possesses this sense of
missionary zeal, and it was confirmed in a report in
'The Times' newspaper on 22nd February 1978 which
quoted the Editor-in-Chief of Pravda as saying, 'Our
aim is propaganda, the propaganda of the party and
state. We do not hide this.' This interpretation
carries with it an educational motive, which is quite
contrary to the interpretation placed upon propaganda
in western, democratic societies. But it is an interpretation which is quite openly proclaimed, it could
be hypothesised that the covert censorship, practised
by editors of the press in 'open' societies, creates
distortion which is only different in kind from that
in the press of authoritarian states. The writings
of Huxley (1964) and in a somewhat different vein
that of Mills (1977) provide interesting commentaries
on the non-rational, propagandist nature of much of
the press in democratic societies.
　　　When we turn to the study of propaganda, we can
notice its far ranging implications; for example,
ideas can be incorporated from psychology, sociology,
politics and communication theory. There have been
numerous definitions proposed, in each case the definition put forward reflects, as one would expect,
the background of the proposer. For instance the
influence of social psychology is reflected in the
definition proposed by Qualter (1962, p. 27) when he
wrote, 'Propaganda is the deliberate attempt by some
individual or group to form, control or alter the
attitudes of other groups by the use of communication
with the intention that in any given situation the
reaction of those so influenced will be that desired
by the propagandist'. It is not quite clear what is
meant by the term communication in this definition,
if what is meant is mediated communication excluding
non-verbal communication, then the definition is inadequate, because propaganda through direct address
plays an important part in political rallies.
　　　An earlier definition, proposed by Lasswell

(1934, p.521), put the issue on a very wide canvas;
he saw propaganda as a technique for influencing
human actions by the manipulation of representations.
This is such a broad definition that it could be seen
to incorporate all forms of art, verbal and visual,
which set out to influence reader/viewer responses.
The visual arts in particular provide ample evidence
of the manipulation of representations, but we do not
normally regard such representations as propagandist,
unless we are aware of, or suspect, political motives.
In fact it is in the intention that we would seek
evidence of propaganda, rather than the representations per se, that is, we would direct our observations more to the content rather than the form, although admittedly the separation of form and content
is more of an abstraction than a fully realisable
possibility.

Perhaps Kecskemeti (1973, p.845), in his attempted theoretical spanning of the issue of propaganda,
put the matter of definition in a useful perspective,
this is how he summed-up the position:

> The proper criteria to set off propagandistic
> from non-propagandistic communications raise
> considerable conceptual problems .... many
> theorists base the distinction on value crit-
> eria (truth versus falsehood, good faith versus
> manipulation, and so on). Most frequently,
> education serves as the paradigm of 'truthful',
> non-propagandistic communications. The employ-
> ment of value criteria, however, has its pit-
> falls; it is only too apt to give the theoret-
> ical discussion of propaganda a propagandistic
> tinge. Among the many definitions cited, the
> most satisfactory ones seem to be given by the
> dictionary. They relate the propagandist's
> intention to a partisan or competitive 'cause'.
> A specific difference between propagandistic
> and non-propagandistic discourse is set forth
> in this way without introducing value criteria.

The central points in Kecskemeti's definition
relate to intention and cause. This underlines the
point made here earlier about the importance of intention, but to this we can now add the notion of
cause, thus we have introduced an ideological note
which we shall take up more fully later in this chapter.

The distinction which seems to be the most appropriate, is the contrast between a dialectical type
of persuasion where inconsistencies in beliefs are
made known with the intention to produce consistency,

131

and a non-dialectical type of persuasion, which
strives for homogeneity and resonance. This latter
type of persuasion is more akin to propaganda than
the former. But then again a great deal of formal
education is carried out in a non-dialectical manner,
but it may, in many instances, preclude the necessity
for homogeneity and resonance between teacher and
taught, thus it is not always propagandistic in the
terms specified before.

On leaving aside the problems of definition, we
can look separately at the structures through which
propaganda is made manifest. We can observe the
forms which it takes in the media, and we can attempt
to specify the underlying psycho-social factors
through which it operates. According to Ellul (1973)
it appears that propaganda is most effective when it
conforms to needs, latent or manifest, needs which
are already existing rather than needs created by
the propagandist. To this extent it is parasitic.
To achieve wide support it has to be couched in
terms or in concepts which find an echo in the greatest number of people, and in consequence it sets its
sights at the lowest common denominator. In order
to avoid argument its content is invariably presented
with a one-sided bias, thus debate is kept to a minimum. Debate would of course weaken the power of
the presenter and introduce a note of equality, which
is the antithesis of authoritarianism.

Perhaps one of the most potent means of propaganda is the utilisation of the social need for affiliation with others. Messages are often couched in
terms appealing to group cohesion and solidarity, to
aims, desires and aspirations as represented by group
norms. The individual can find himself being addressed in personal terms, but in terms that only have
value in relation to a group. The social need to
affiliate or to 'belong' to groups, or to identify
with particular others, brings in its train group
distinctions and contrasts. The togetherness generated by group affiliation leads to social homogeneity,
to a lessening of distinctions and a strengthening
of similarities. On the other hand, inter-group
contrasts can be made with stigma attached to other
groups. On the larger scale of society at the national level we can note the stress on common factors;
national appeals are intended to produce sympathy by
the mere factor of belonging to that particular nation.

It is not only social homogeneity that is utilised in propaganda, there is also the fact of message
homogeneity, the repetition of messages bearing the
same theme, expressing the same positive or negative

emotional attitude. It is assumed that by constant,
undeviating repetition, resistance to the theme will
be lowered, or conversely, strengthened when agree-
ment has been attained. So we should expect to find
media homogeneity in those countries where the central government is the sole agent for the propagation
of news. Likewise we should expect to find in those
countries with a 'free' press that the characteristics
of a newspaper could be defined by its particular
brand of homogeneity. We have mentioned the importance of 'needs', the influence of 'belongingness',
and the utilisation of homogeneity as key aspects of
propaganda, but to this list we must add a further
item, that of 'truth'. Without at least minimal
truth in the message, propaganda loses credibility.
This is contrary to the often repeated statement that
propaganda is all lies; if it were, it would fail in
its objective.

In attempting to assess the effectiveness of
propaganda it is difficult to disentangle all the
influences from other sources which bear upon the
individual. Experimental work with small groups can
throw-up interesting ideas and generate useful hypotheses, but the forces which shape attitudes have
many tributaries, and sometimes long histories. In
deterministic terms, Ellul (1973) viewed the creation
of technological society as the main contributory
factor in the emergence of propaganda, a society in
which people come to be conditioned to a 'need for
propaganda'. In fact, he viewed propaganda in such
broad terms that he believed that early experiences
in life can be considered as preparation for propaganda. Apparently what is meant here is that children are in a non-dialectical relationship with their
superiors, thus they are merely given information or
commands. Industrial society, to Ellul, is one where
pseudo-needs are created for pseudo-satisfactions.
Such an interpretation places propaganda more in the
framework of advertising and less in the traditional
approach to propaganda which is more in the direction
of politics. It would be reasonable to infer that
industrialisation and urbanisation have produced
changes which favour the growth of propaganda, but it
could be argued that propaganda is more of an agency
for conservation than change. Critical reactions to
propaganda require critical people, and critical people require familiarity with argument. Thus resistance to propaganda is a problem for education in its
broadest sense.

Propaganda is not an isolated phenomenon existing at a distance, its power resides in its ability

to tap human strengths and frailties. An awareness
of this situation can aid the propagandist in his
purposes; conversely, it can aid the propagandee to
build resistance to it. The insistence of propaganda
is heightened in modern, technological society, but
its deeper significance is in the ideology by which
it is sustained.

Ideology

It is a fact that man, in the singular, can only
view the world from a particular frame of reference;
it is at best only a partial, segmental view and thus
open to bias. Frames of reference are employed in
the interpretation of sensory stimuli, in which case
it is a psycho-perceptual phenomenon; in addition they
are employed in the interpretation of social life,
in which case the ground is that of ideology. Barthes
(1968), using the language of the semiologist, defined
ideology as the form of the signifieds of connotation.
But Althusser (1977) applied a more deterministic
definition; to him, ideology utilises forms endowed
with historical significance in the shape of images,
myths, ideas or concepts serving a practico-social
function, rather than a theoretical function.

Because man can only obtain a segmental view of
the world (although as a philosopher he tries to do
otherwise), and because he forms his ideologies from
a particular point of view, we can appreciate the
almost inevitability of bias. And bias, as we know,
runs directly through most aspects of organised persuasive appeals, through advertising and through
propaganda; hence the study of ideology is germane
to the study of the processes of persuasion in more
ways than one. Through ideology we can focus upon
the frameworks, real or idealised, which play a part
in man's social conditioning. We can look at the way
in which the style of life, particularly that engendered by modern technological society, creates special biases. However the creation of bias is not a
straightforward process, it has to contend with pre-
existing frames of reference which can act to reject
incoming ideas, or at least test their validity against existing ideas. Not only that, if the ideas
emanate from a source lacking in credibility, then
the message itself will be considered as suspect; the
work of Hovland (1957) on the credibility of communicators makes useful reading in this context. Likewise, the general ineffectiveness of British and German propaganda during the Second World War could be
attributed to the fact that the recipients of the propaganda did not accord credibility to the source.

As has been pointed out in this book on a number
of occasions, persuasion is not a one-way affair from
sender to pliant receiver, it has to contend with a
variety of counter-influences, the most important
being the individual's own stock of psychological
defences. With the emergence of industrial society
life is lived at a more symbolic level, and a greater
distance has been introduced between cause and effect
in the individual's day-to-day activities. Via the
realm of the symbolic, the persuader can, metaphorically speaking, play a game using images already
formed in the minds of the recipients, it is a game
calling upon man's potential for creating connotations. But unless he, the advertiser or propagandist,
is aware of particular cultural or sub-cultural codes,
his message may take a different route to the one
intended. As Eco (1977, p.139) pointed out, the
multiplicity of codes, contexts, and circumstances
mean that the same message can be decoded from different points of view and by reference to diverse
systems of conventions. The basic denotation of a
particular sign or symbol can be understood as the
sender intended it, but different connotations can
be attributed to it simply because the receiver follows a different path to the one envisaged by the sender,
and both paths might be quite legitimate in a shared
or common culture.

Of considerable interest to the theme of persu-
sion and ideology is the work of Marcuse (1968) whose
book 'One Dimensional Man' bears the sub-title, the
ideology of industrial society. To Marcuse, one of
the paramount aspects of modern industrial society
is the way in which needs are manipulated, or purpor-
ted to be manipulated, and this of course is the territory of the professional persuader. According to
Marcuse, needs may be true or false; from his perspective, true needs are those related to survival,
such as food, clothing and shelter; conversely, false
needs are not related to physical survival, but to
the needs of survival in social life. However, through
social conditioning, a paradox can exist in that false
needs can be felt as true needs when it is not understood that the source is in society as such and not
in the individual as a fact of nature. This paradox
was neatly put by Marcuse when he wrote (p.24):

.... in the most highly developed areas of contemporary society, the transplantation of social
into individual needs is so effective that the
difference between them seems to be purely theoretical. Can one really distinguish between the

mass media as instruments of information and
entertainment, and as agents of manipulation
and indoctrination? Between the automobile as
nuisance and convenience? We are again con-
fronted with one of the most vexing aspects of
advanced industrial civilisation; the rational
character of its irrationality... The people
recognise themselves in their commodities; they
find their soul in their automobile, hi-fi set,
split-level home, kitchen equipment. The very
mechanism which ties the individual to his society has changed, and social control is anchored
in the new needs which it has produced.

Seen in these terms man is caught in a kind of
trap which is not of his own making but that of society, demands are made by technological society which
follow from its nature, and which are necessary for
its continuation. The implication here is that man
is unable to distinguish between true and false needs,
and even when he is able to do so, he will tend to
give priority to society's demands. This seems to
be an overstatement, most people are quite capable
of distinguishing primary or biological needs. The
issue is more about the deliberate charging of secondary, non-biological needs with scales of values
created by society, thus opening up the prospect of
the non-essential, survivalwise, being perceived as
essential, socialwise.
The ploy that persuaders can adopt is to heighten
false needs and to suggest their indispensability.
To the extent that such suggestions are effective in
achieving their purpose, it could be argued that false
needs can become true needs. But there is another
consideration to bear in mind, man has always had
social-psychological needs to satisfy, they exist
in primitive societies, but they are 'traded-on' more
explicitly in modern technological society. They
become functional, or practico-social needs which
regulate man's part in society, they create a functional ideology.
From functional ideology develops functional
language, a language which supports the needs of
technological society in general rather than the
individual in particular; it eschews the critical
and the dialectical, it establishes strong ethical
distinctions between rights and wrongs, it tends to
be concrete, and as Marcuse suggested, the 'thing'
identified with its function is more real than the
'thing' distinguished from its function, and the linguistic expression of this identification creates a

basic vocabulary and syntax which is opposed to differentiation, separation and distinction. Here we
can see echoes of mythology, the identification of
symbol with thing symbolized and the blurring of distinctions.

Functional ideology is often presented in borrowed terms, commercial art borrows from the fine arts,
but whereas fine art may deal with that which is
problematic, commercial art tends to be positive and
affirmative. Avoidance of the negative epitomises
functional ideology, it is antithetical to argument,
and hence to use the term made popular through the
work of Marcuse, it perpetuates 'one dimensional man',
a man to whom distinctions, opposites and negations
are anathema, who strives towards conformity and unanimity of goals and purposes. In the work of Schein
and others (1961) on coercive persuasion, we can note
a similar insistence on unanimity as a method for
inculcating a particular ideology, in this instance
it was Marxist-Leninism. In this case it was prisoners of war who were subjected to attempted indoctrination, and they had no freedom to leave their restricted environment. However, by the same token,
Marcuse believed people in general are trapped within
a consciousness which is false and representative of
values implanted by society, thus offering only the
illusion of freedom.

Both advertising and propaganda are concerned
with values; in the case of advertising it is the
values of products and services, and in the case of
propaganda it is the values of political parties or
governments. They both set out to shape values in
particular ways, ways which suit their ideologies.
The term ideology has become associated with oppression, oppression of the weak by the strong, this
bears some element of truth, but only when it is prefixed by the word dominant. Ideology is an inevitable
and normal complement to man's existence; as was
stated earlier, man, in the singular, can only obtain
a partial or segmental view of the world. This fact
also applied to man in his pre-technological condition,
but with increasing use of artefacts and the greater
distance between man and nature a false consciousness
has greater scope to fit into man's scheme of things.
Hence the attraction of Marcuse's notion of false
consciousness which can be discovered in the relationship between the law of things and the law of society

Persuasion, at least commercial or propagandistic
persuasion of the non-rational kind, tends to emphasise the fusion between individuals, products and

ideals, it is a kind of false consciousness which bears strong similarities to magic as described by social anthropologists. Hence it could be hypothesised that pre-technological man and technological man share the same common trait, and this trait is man as symbol user which makes possible the fusion or identity of representation and thing represented, in semiological terms, the fusion of signifier and signified.

Historical factors bear down upon people, they provide forms or frames of reference which could be termed their ideology. They provide reference points for interpretation; just as in map-making, co-ordinates are necessary for position finding, so ideological co-ordinates provide reference points for social life, the accuracy or otherwise of the co-ordinates is another question. In terms of persuasion, the intention is to give a particular or partisan structure, this may be done overtly, for example the advertisement which declares itself for what it is, or it may be done covertly, through an imaginary relationship which can be misconstrued as a real relationship, an ideological fiction. Perhaps we should end this chapter with a word of warning provided by Althusser, who saw ideology not as an aberration or a contingent excresence of history, but as a structure essential to the historical life of societies. The issue then becomes not just that of ideology per se, this is an indispensable condition of man as symbol user, but about the ways that particular ideologies are formed and maintained. In modern society they are formed and maintained by social conditions which include family, school, group affiliations and work situations, plus the influences derived from various media.

SUMMARY

1. Commercial persuasion is an economic issue which may draw upon psychological and sociological needs.

2. Advertising that appeals to transformation by identification with fabricated images can be considered in terms of mythology, particularly magic.

3. Covert appeals can be analysed in at least two separate ways: (i) through Freudian psychological explanations; (ii) through Veblenian sociological explanations.

4. Appraisal of the persuasive power of advertising needs to consider the effects, not only present- ation variables.

5. Propaganda is most effective when it conforms to existing needs, whether they be latent or manifest.

6. Because man can only obtain a restricted view of the world, he tends to introduce bias. Hence ideologies are partial to this limitation.

7. The form and order in which life is lived serves as a reference point. This point of reference can produce 'false consciousness' in which the non-essential, survivalwise, can be perceived as essential, socialwise.

REFERENCES

ALTHUSSER, L. (1977) For Marx. London: NLB.

BARTHES, R. (1968) Elements of Semiology. New York: Hill & Wang.

BERGER, J. (1972) Ways of Seeing. London: B.B.C. and Harmondsworth: Penguin.

ECO. U. (1977) A Theory of Semiotics. London: Macmillan.

ELLUL, J. (1973) Propaganda. New York: Vintage Books.

FRAZER, J.G. (1935) The Golden Bough: a study in magic and religion. London: Macmillan.

GOSSAGE, H.L. (1967) The gilded bough: magic and advertising. In Matson, F.W. and Montagu, A.(eds.) The Human Dialogue: perspectives on communication. New York: The Free Press. pp.363-370.

HOVLAND, C.I. (ed.) (1957) The Order of Presentation in Persuasion. New Haven: Yale University Press.

HUXLEY, A. (1964) Brave New World Revisited. London: Chatto & Windus.

KECSKEMETI, P. (1975) Propaganda. In de Sola Pool,I. and Schramm, W. (eds.) Handbook of Communication. Chicago: Rand McNally, pp. 844-870.

LASSWELL, H.D. (1934) Propaganda. In the Encyclo- pedia of the Social Sciences, vol.12, New York: Macmillan, pp. 521-528.

MacKAY, D. (1969) Information, Mechanism and Meaning. Cambridge, Mass.: The M.I.T. Press.

MARCUSE, H. (1968) One Dimensional Man. London: Sphere Books.

MILLS, C.W. (1977) The Power Elite. Oxford: Oxford University Press.

PACKARD, V. (1962) The Hidden Persuaders. Harmondsworth: Penguin.

QUALTER, T.H. (1962) Propaganda and Psychological
    Warfare. New York: Random House.
SCHEIN, E.H. SCHNEIER, I. and BARKER, C.H. (1961)
    Coercive Persuasion. New York: W.W. Norton & Co.
VEBLEN, T. (1970) The Theory of the Leisure Class.
    London: Unwin.

Chapter Thirteen

RESISTANCE TO PERSUASION

It is proper in a book on persuasion to draw attention to the various manifest and latent sources and
avenues of persuasion. It is also proper to make
known the resistance which exists or can be created
to persuasion; in this chapter we set out to make
known the bases of such resistance. Contemporary
western life faces the individual with persuasive
messages from a variety of sources and through a
variety of media. Some advertisements offer images
of ourselves in idealised forms, with the intention
that through imagination we 'put ourselves in the
picture' achieving a kind of transformation through
the product or service offered in the advertisement,
while other advertisements may be more mundane,
explicitly making their case without concealed or
covert intentions. In social, non-mediated situations we may also find ourselves faced with information bearing persuasive intent. Yet despite the
blandishments of advertisements and the influence of
others, we know that we possess certain powers of
resistance. Resistance can be proportional to the
freedom at one's disposal to do or think otherwise,
and to the consequences that one is prepared to
tolerate as the result of one's actions.
    The systematic study of resistance to persuasion
has interesting antecedents, particularly we can
notice the concern felt about the possibility of
organised indoctrination. The Korean War and its
aftermath aroused special interest owing to the attempted indoctrination of American prisoners of war
(the treatment of German prisoners by their British
captors at the time of the second world war was described in more gentle terms, it was known as re-
education). From this period, experimental studies
were carried out to test the effects of alternative
strategies in preparing people to resist messages

with strong persuasive biases. While later, in the field of media studies, the work of Baggaley and Duck (1976) demonstrated how an awareness of the techniques and devices used in television production can render transparent its covert potential for influence; in the language of communication theory, one can learn to decode the process and thus expose the meta-messages contained in the presentation.

However, while the effects of learning to recognise and decode persuasive communications may indeed be beneficial and efficacious, it appears that some of the most potent factors contributing to resistance to persuasion are those relating to credibility, to prior commitments to established beliefs, and to the effect of belonging to particular groups.

Credibility

Throughout the literature on resistance to persuasion, the concept of credibility stands out with special significance. A credible communicator can influence acceptance (persuasion), whereas a non-credible communicator can have the reverse effect, he can cause resistance to the contents of the message. From this principle we can understand why so much of advertising fails to achieve the goals or aims of its progenitors - people do not automatically give credence to the source, they generally possess sufficient discrimination to be able to differentiate between sources. From the work of Hovland (1953:1957) and his team at Yale University, it was found that a highly credible performer, or one so perceived, had a substantially greater immediate effect on audience opinion than one with low credibility. It was found that people with high credibility have the effect of influencing their audience to accept the conclusions advocated, rather than concentrating upon the logic of the contents of the message. However, this did show up as a kind of short-term effect; with the passage of time the contents themselves became the centre of focus, thus suggesting that for long-term effects it is the contents rather than the performer or communicator that gains ascendency. In other words, rhetoric accompanied by belief in the credibility of the rhetorician is not sustained if the contents of the message are found to be untenable. Another factor is whether the idea or theme of a message is continually associated with the original source or not, and whether that same source is still perceived as being credible.

A further point is intention; irrespective of the credibility of the source, if people possess little or no intention to commit the contents of a message to long-term memory, then its long-term effects are reduced accordingly. The issue is one of incentive, and this is where the persuaders of commercial intent find their niche, they set out to provide incentives.

Learning

The effectiveness of communication can be judged as a particular type of learning; likewise, as persuasion is extricably bound to communication it also has a learning dimension, but generally speaking it is a one-way form of communication, i.e. it is non-dialectical. Furthermore it tends not to aim for concept learning, which requires the learner to generalise to other situations. Far from it, the tendency in most forms of commercial persuasion is to particularise, to deliberately exclude competing products, except for the purpose of showing them in a lesser light, to provide a set (to use the terminology of set theory) in which only the proffered product can belong, a kind of enoblement by exclusion.

It can also be noted that the success of a persuasive communication can be judged or measured by its ability to confer resistance to subsequent competing information. Here we can invoke the work of Schein (1961) who formulated extensive ideas on the nature of resistance and non-resistance in his studies of American prisoners at the time of the Korean conflict, or more correctly in its aftermath. These prisoners were subjected to systematic attempts at indoctrination, of course in the eyes of their captors it would be seen more as an attempt at corrective education. However what is important is that the environment was controlled in such a way that controls could be exercised over a variety of variables, a kind of control that makes possible an analysis in terms of S-R psychology. Schein, however, interpreted the control methods in more sociological terms. He wrote, 'This program should not be viewed as a collection of specific techniques routinely applied, but rather as the creation of a whole set of social conditions within which certain techniques operated.'

The important point here is that it was a social situation which could be, and in fact was, subject to systematic manipulation. The aim of the captors was to create new beliefs and attitudes in their captives. From this period the term brainwashing was introduced into the English language. In the Chinese language it has a healthy or cleansing connotation, implying the cleansing of the mind, hence brain-washing; in

English of course it has taken on the opposite meaning, the sinister 'ring' of indoctrination. Such
is the way that language can shift to other connotations when it is tied to particular events or contexts.

In all closed situations the individual is
forced into compliance which he would not necessarily
countenance in 'open situations'. Of course there
are always exceptions to this rule, but generally
speaking the majority of people take the line of
least resistance when they are faced with few or no
alternatives. In such situations people are forced
into a dependence relationship which the controllers
of the situation can use to their own advantage, that
is, to produce behavioural responses in line with
their own particular beliefs. Not only responses,
but beliefs of a particular kind can be aimed at;
this was the intention of the Chinese captors, an
intention to inculcate beliefs of the ruling party.
The captives faced, as do all captives in all places
and at all times, a dependence upon their captors
for sustenance and other primary human needs; in
such situations, acceptance of authority is imposed.
But in these situations more subtle factors can be
brought to bear upon the reluctant prisoners, for
instance the Chinese captors used the repetition
and pacing of demands, forced constant participation,
and the deliberate insertion of new ideas into old
and meaningful contexts. This can be related to the
anchoring of ideas which was discussed in the earlier
chapter on memory.

Another important factor was the pressure to
collaborate, but collaboration did not mean that
indoctrination actually occurred. Schein recognised
that it is difficult to measure the latent effects
of such experiences. In fact most prisoners chose
not to remain in China after the Korean War. During
their captivity social isolation was sometimes created, but even so, such isolation was never suffic-
iently extended to make the prisoners completely
dependent upon their captors. Also, despite the
care taken by the captors to establish a fine degree
of social control, the prisoners in general were
not won over to the beliefs which their captors
desired to inculcate. It could be argued that the
low standard of material life in the camps and the
impoverished surroundings gave the men an example
of life which was materially inferior to that to
which they were accustomed in their own country.
And in such circumstances, ideological conditioning,
or more accurately attempted ideological conditioning,

144

faces strong resistance. In fact when the prisoners
were repatriated to their own country, they tended
to express strong anti-Communist feelings. However
there were some conversions; a small number of the
returning prisoners were found to have changed their
ideological stance in the direction of their captors.
Collaboration with their captors was one measure used
to assess persuasive influences on the prisoners, but
such collaboration that took place could be attributed as much to ensuing material benefits as to a
change in political views.

Habits

The example given of attempted indoctrination, more
colourfully known as brainwashing, or more kindly
interpreted as re-education, gives insight into a
number of psychological and social-psychological
factors which may play a part in persuasion. But
what is also clear is that people are not as susceptible to persuasion as the popular literature on the
subject would indicate; the work of Packard (1962)
can be cited as an example of popular literature.
We can also take note of the study made by McGinnies
(1974) relating to the newspaper strike in New York
in 1963; during that strike the only paper available
on the stands for sale was one that conflicted with
the ideological perspective of the majority of busi-
nessmen, and although many such people bought the
one available paper during the strike, they did,
nevertheless, soon revert to their habitual choice
when the strike was over. The implication here is
that, as in the case of the Korean War prisoners,
a temporary situation, at least one which is perceived as such, does not necessarily have long-term
effects. What it does demonstrate is that reading
habits, like eating habits, are sometimes satisfied
by what is on offer.
It is to the role of underlying attitudes or
dispositions that we must direct our attention for
a fuller understanding of the nature of resistance
to persuasion. Situational factors do play an important part, but a part which is also influenced by what
any one individual brings in the way of dispositions
to the present from the past, a past which frames the
way that the present in interpreted, hence influencing current responses. For example in the case cited
of the American prisoners in the hands of their
Chinese captors, they brought with them into captivity a psychological and social conditioning peculiar
to their upbringing. Therefore at a manifest level
they could display a surface impression of acceptance

of their captors ideology, but at the latent level
a different set of beliefs could be operating. As
a result of the calculated attempt at indoctrination
of these American prisoners, interest was focused
upon the possibility of experimentally controlling
various ways in which people can be prepared to face
persuasive messages.

Pre-training

Here we can direct attention towards the work of
McGuire (1973) who developed what has commonly come
to be known as inoculation theory. The term inoculation is by analogy to medical practice, i.e. the
injection of a small dose of a particular disease
to ward off the chance of a full attack at a later
time. In the McGuire example the idea is that a
mild attack on an accepted belief will stimulate an
individual to create defences against subsequent
larger attacks, thus we can see the analogy with
medical practice. The contents of the messages used
by McGuire were cultural truisms, that is, beliefs
which are held to be true without question, for
example, the belief that brushing one's teeth is a
necessary and efficient form of dental hygiene, an
idea that is usually accepted on trust without further
questioning.

The main result of McGuire's research was to demonstrate that people who were supplied with evidence
that refuted the truisms used in his experiments were
more able to resist subsequent messages than were
people who has been supplied with supporting evidence,
i.e. evidence which supported the truisms to which
they were already attached. The evidence from this
research suggests that in preparing people who are
likely to become involved in situations where their
cherished beliefs, faulty or otherwise, are likely
to come under attack, then it is better for them to
be familiar with facing arguments than run counter
to their established beliefs. Of course it would be
desirable for all educational systems to so challenge
their students that they are familiar with argument
and counter-argument as a necessary part of preparation for life. However, to return to McGuire's
research, this was carried out after the Korean War,
so we are entitled to ask on what grounds did the
American prisoners, who had not been subjected to
systematic pre-training in resisting challenges to
their political beliefs, rely for refuting the projected beliefs of their captors? It could be argued
that the nature of the attacks on their beliefs was
inadequate, that they contained sufficient inaccuracies

not to bring the questioning process into operation, thus, in this instance, pre-treatment or 'inoculation' was not essential. Acquiescence would be at surface level with no ideological conflict being present at the deeper level; acquiescence becomes necessary for survival for most normal people when they find themselves in situations of forced compliance, situations where no options are presented.

Returning to the general findings of McGuire's work, we can note that the actual techniques of building resistance produce different effects, for instance, reading (termed passive defence) was found to be superior to writing (termed active defence) in developing resistance to attack by familiar counter-arguments, but active defence was found to be superior in protecting people against novel counter-arguments. Also, although it was found that supportive material was less effective than argument by refutation, the supportive material did confer benefits in increasing resistance to later persuasion. In addition, it has been found that forewarning of an attack on a person's beliefs confers a certain amount of resistance to subsequent persuasion. In military terms one could say that defences are marshalled.

The evidence from research in this field coupled with the work reported by Schein is both interesting and instructive, providing some hope against the fears of human frailty in the face of various forms of attempted indoctrination in society at large, through the press and in real life situations. It demonstrates the ways in which people can be prepared to meet persuasive messages, although as mentioned earlier one would assume that a sound education would make the necessary preparations.

Groups

Persuasion, although it may be an individual affair, is also an issue related to man's existence with and for others. McGuire extended his research to look at the effect of group influence, and he found that if a person is made aware that others hold the same belief as himself there is a tendency for his adherence to the belief to increase or be strengthened. Group and situational variants are involved here. The forging of links has an anchoring effect, to use a maritime metaphor; we have already seen how mental organisation in learning and remembering is influenced by anchoring ideas and concepts. Now we can see that connecting or identifying with others has a similar anchoring effect. Links can be forged at a social level, thus stabilising the individual's self-judgement

in a wider setting. It is interesting to note that
a person does not necessarily have to be in the
actual presence of others in a group for anchoring
to take place, the group can be merely a reference
group, the kind of group that one can aspire to
without being an actual member. Here we can see the
use of certain groups being put forward as reference
groups, groups which purport to set particular standards to which others may aspire, a kind of persuasion
by example. There are many examples of the commercial exploitation of this effect; we can note the way
in which certain advertisements present prestige
groups as a source of other reference, albeit an
idealised reference.

Distraction

Research carried out by Festinger and Maccoby (1964)
and later by Vohs and Garrett (1968) into the effects
of distraction during the reception of persuasive
messages is of particular interest to our theme.
They found that people who are subjected to some
form of distraction during the reception of persuasive messages are more prone to accept their contents. Given the limited capacity of the brain to
process information, the implication is that distraction makes counter-arguing less likely. In
information theory terms, the limited capacity to
deal with the totality of presented information sets
up a condition whereby some information is processed
at the expense of other, that is, when a person is
in a condition of overload. Distraction can be seen
therefore as a 'loading' device taking up the capacity which might otherwise be available for counter-
arguing.

We are now in a position to see that resistance
to persuasion is quite a complicated process. There
are the psychological factors which we have just mentioned, and the social factors made explicit in the
work of Schein. In a general sense these two factors
cannot be entirely separated, people do, inevitably,
bring their personal dispositions into social relationships, thus producing a certain influence on
the interactions that take place. On the other hand,
social factors serve to influence the behaviour of
the individual, irrespective of his or her psychological make-up. It takes a strong personality to
stand aside from the totality of group influence.

Reactance

So far we have been taking ideas from research in
the general area of resistance to persuasion, but

there is another important route that we can follow
in our quest for understanding, in particular we can
take a look at the related work of Brehm (1966) who
was concerned with what he termed reactance. He
produced a theory of reactance which has two main
elements, namely freedom and importance. We can
relate reactance to resistance.

According to Brehm, the importance of the freedom to take a given position is a direct function of
how closely that position represents what one believes
to be correct. For example, if both the freedom and
importance are high, maximal reactance to persuasive
appeals is likely to follow. Thus we can see that
in closed situations, such as those that applied in
the prisons where the American troops were held in
Korea, and of course in all prison situations there
is very little freedom, and therefore we would expect
that compliance or non-reactance would be the norm.
However, when freedom of choice is available and
importance is attached to the issue presented, then
we would expect maximal reactance.

It could be argued that individuals exist in
a constant state of latent resistance to influence,
that tacit knowledge is brought into play on the
receipt of communications, whether they are intended
to be persuasive or otherwise. To consider fully
the nature of resistance it would appear to be necessary to make a careful analysis of the tacit dimension, here the work of Polanyi (1966) is of particular relevance. In fact the major works on research
into resistance to persuasion touch upon the problem,
but they fail to make explicit the centrality of the
tacit dimension, or to put the matter another way,
insufficient attention is paid to those latent forces
which contribute to resistance. By directing attention to latent factors we can begin to find an explanation for the reason why people, who are exposed to
so much explicit persuasion in contemporary life
through the press and television, are generally not
moved to change their beliefs or responses. Explicit
appeals are subjected to latent scrutiny which may
set in motion a kind of censorship or non-approval
without a great deal of conscious effort. So the
bombardment of advertisements upon the senses, particularly the visual sense in the case of television,
can be seen to affect the immediate perceptual input,
but fail to make a lasting register when passed to
the deeper, more permanent level, wherein latent
appraisal is made.

In reviewing the various pieces of published
work on resistance to persuasion, one can be struck

by a particular paradox which none of the researchers
has commented upon, namely, that encouraging resistance to persuasion can itself by considered a form
of persuasion. To persuade somebody to resist is to
cause a particular kind of influence, an influence
stemming from an external agency.

The various sub-theories on resistance display
the particular concerns of the social scientists
engaged in this field. Therefore the questions which
have been posed have reflected the particular concerns of the researchers; for instance hypotheses
directed towards the effects of the structure of
messages produce theories in line with communication
models of the traditional Shannon and Weaver type.
Whereas the view from the bridge of the social-
psychologist has given an orientation towards group
influences. In viewing the various contributions to
the study of resistance, the directness of Brehm's
reactance theory seems to offer the most elegant
model. In the first place it can be related to the
responses of normal people in normal situations, it
also posits a state of natural resistance, a resistance found in the nature of man without the need for
specifying controlling forces. The twin concepts of
'freedom' and 'importance' can be grasped for their
relevance without invoking elaborate experimental
evidence, although for those wishing such evidence,
the work of Brehm provides facts to bolster his
theory.

Returning to the concept of 'freedom', we know
intuitively that with no freedom of choice we are
not even in a position to react, except in the sense
of the human propensity to imagine and thus conceive
of mental alternatives. This is the sense in which
Jean-Paul Sartre (1972) conceives man's absolute
freedom, a freedom which can transcend any imposed
restrictions. However, when we leave the realms of
imagination, when we come down to earth and the
practicalities of everyday life, reactance is at a
minimum when alternatives are not presented. On the
other hand, when the individual has a great amount
of freedom, he can afford to react to persuasive
messages which impinge upon his choice. So choice
then is a kind of freedom, a freedom to choose from
alternatives; the greater the alternatives the greater
the choice, and the greater reactance that we could
expect to any one alternative which is not desired.

Running parallel with the concept of freedom
is that of importance; things or ideas of low importance tend not to generate reactance; it is as if
individuals are not prepared to expend mental energy
on things which are of little importance to them.

Conversely, things of importance gain attention, gaining priority amongst alternatives; thus ideas attacking existing ideas which are held in some esteem or importance, will tend to produce reactance.

Further analysing the literature in this field, we may be drawn to the conclusion that there is nothing particularly new about the employment of various techniques of persuasion and counter-persuasion. As Schein noted there was nothing new or terrifying about the specific techniques employed by the Chinese on their American captives, we can observe that similar techniques are widely used in psychiatry. The novelty lay in the combination and the purposes for which they were used.

Within the wider framework of the study of persuasion, when we take in a historical perspective, we can see attempted manipulative or conditioning techniques in operation through past centuries and in many parts of the world. In particular, many attempts at religious conversion can be seen to use conditioning techniques; graphic examples are given in the work of Sargant (1957).

The final paradox is that it could be considered to be unwise to resist all forms of persuasion and influence. Much of persuasion could be considered to be ethically acceptable, for example government attempts through advertising to encourage people not to smoke. It appears that the issue of persuasion and resistance should not be judged solely as an abstraction, that consideration needs to be given to the contents. It could be argued that certain contents are ethically acceptable, and that others are not, even when the conditions of persuasion are the same.

Alerting the reader to the ideas discussed here puts the problem into a wider context, usually it is discussed in pejorative terms. What needs stressing is the power of latent resistance, what is usually stressed is the overt potential of persuasion. Surface level analyses of persuasion highlight the form of persuasive messages, they rarely take into account the covert or latent defences which can be marshalled, often without the conscious awareness of the persuadee. Sartre saw man's ultimate freedom as lying in his ability or propensity to imagine, an imagination that is not constrained by any external agency. Perhaps we can add that when given freedom of choice man can also resist or react to the many influences that bear down upon him. Finally we may ask, is it always wise to resist influence? Would we not at times be poorer for resisting? These are ethical questions, therefore we need specific instances on which to base our judgements. What is of paramount importance is the freedom of individuals to make their own decisions.

SUMMARY

1. The credibility of the source plays an important part in gaining acceptance of ideas, but for lasting influence, it is the message itself, in its own right, that provides greater impact.

2. Arguments requiring refutation rather than those giving support provide a sounder foundation for resistance to later attacks.

3. Group affiliation either real or imagined (referenced) is a source of influence in self-judgement.

4. Distraction can be a covert way of reducing resistance to persuasive messages, it can reduce counter-arguing.

5. The stronger beliefs are tied to some other permanent reference system the stronger the will to resist current influences.

6. Resistance to persuasion increases in proportion to the degree of freedom available to the individual, and to the importance attached to the issue at stake.

7. Resistance to persuasion raises ethical issues, it could be argued that in certain instances resistance to persuasion is not beneficial.

REFERENCES

BAGGALEY, J. and DUCK, S. (1976) Dynamics of Television. Farnborough, Hants.: Saxon House.
BREHM, J.W. (1966) A Theory of Psychological Reactance. New York: Academic Press.
FESTINGER, L. and MACCOBY, N. (1964) On resistance to persuasive communications. Journal of Abnormal and Social Psychology. Vol.68, No. 4, pp. 359-366.
HOVLAND, C.I. (1953) Communication and Persuasion. New Haven: Yale University Press.
HOVLAND, C.I. (1957) The Order of Presentation in Persuasion. New Haven: Yale University Press.
McGINNIES, E. (1974) Cognitive and behavioral approaches to persuasion. In Silverstein, A. (ed.) Human Communication: theoretical explorations. New York: John Wiley, pp. 185-201

McGUIRE, W.J. (1973) Inducing resistance to persuasion. In Warren, N. & Jahoda, M. (eds.) Attitudes. Harmondsworth: Penguin. pp.139-163.

PACKARD, V. (1962) The Hidden Persuaders. Harmondsworth: Penguin.

POLANYI, M. (1966) The Tacit Dimension. New York: Doubleday.

SARGANT, W. (1957) Battle for the Mind. London: Heinemann.

SARTRE, J - P. (1972) The Psychology of Imagination. London: Methuen.

SCHEIN, E.H. (1961) Coercive Persuasion. New York: W.W. Norton & Co.

VOHS, J.L.and GARRETT, R.L. (1968) Resistance to persuasion: an integrative framework. Public Opinion Quarterly, Vol. 33, pp.445-452.

Chapter Fourteen

CONCLUDING CONSIDERATIONS

In this book the processes of persuasion have been
viewed from a wide perspective. These processes
concern the individual as a psychological entity,
and as a social being; they also concern the means
whereby man communicates with man, either directly
through spoken language or through other media. Thus
it can be seen that the study of persuasion has extensive ramifications, extending from factors within
the individual to those which pattern the ways in
which society is organised, and the ways in which
communication flows between its members. In fact
a fully comprehensive study, taking it to the nth
degree, would be so embracing that it would need to
be issued in volumes. Particular subject specialists
could each make extensive contributions; for example,
from psychology, sociology, semiology and politics.
However, there is a need to see relationships across
these academic boundaries, and one of the purposes
of this book was to trace some of these links.
    Certain critical facts stand out, one is that
persuasion may be employed to produce change or to
resist change. In the first instance its purpose is
anti-conservative, pushing against that part of man's
nature which seeks a state of equilibrium; while in
the second instance its purpose is one of conservation, directed towards the maintenance of the status
quo. An analysis of the methods used in advertising
and propaganda shows that either direction may be
employed according to their appropriateness in particular situations or campaigns. However, the ultimate
ground on which persuasion works is the ground of man's
mind, but this is not a 'tabula rasa'. Any one individual carries his own personal and social history
which biases his perceptions and conceptions. Therefore any study of persuasion which fails to take
account of psychological and societal factors is limited.

Likewise, account needs to be taken of the codes of society, the semiological factors through which signification is given and obtained.

Persuasion presents two faces; the overt, as in the case of declared advertisements, and the covert, in which case its intentions are concealed; the concealment of intentions may be a deliberate act of deception, in which case the origins and/or purposes are withheld, or, it may represent the structure of society which bears upon its members in a persuasive way without their cognizance of the fact.

Persuasion presents a paradox which is contained within the nature of man as a language user. Natural language is composed of words which can be used to express facts and words which can be used to express emotions; and, in face-to-face interaction, it can be issued forth with the persuasive richness of non-verbal forms of communication. Moreover, these persuasive influences may be delivered beyond the conscious awareness of both sender and receiver. Both in his rationality and non-rationality man can be persuasive; rational arguments can cause change in beliefs and hence attitudes; likewise, emotive appeals without any clear logic can also cause a change in attitudes, through a change in values. In practice, however, the logical and the emotive are generally fellow travellers, the major distinction being the weightings they carry on particular occasions.

What is abundantly clear is that persuasion is a multi-variable theme for study; it takes place against a number of psychological variables which may facilitate or hinder its intentions; it takes place against norms given by society, its groups or sub-groups; and it takes place through communicative links which, themselves, conform to pre-existing codes and code structures. Armed with this knowledge, we can see why propaganda directed at other alien societies (e.g. British and German propaganda during the Second World War; Cruickshank, 1977; Balfour,1979) was mainly ineffectual, because it was unable to satisfy the many separate conditions which give credibility to the whole. Analysis of propaganda is invariably directed to its form and control without reference to its effectiveness, yet, in the final analysis, it is effectiveness that counts. The rest may be merely a game that propagandists play. This scepticism was echoed in the review of Balfour's book 'Propaganda in War', 1939-1945' by A.J.P. Taylor; he wrote, 'I regard wartime propaganda with complete scepticism except as a means of keeping intellectuals out of mischief. Its function is that of the rope

Boswell was instructed to pull during a storm in the
Hebrides; this was quite useless but it gave Boswell
a sensation of doing something.'

However, experimentation has provided guidelines which point to the effects of different forms
of message structure (Hovland, 1957) and the effects
of various manipulative devices which television
producers can employ (Baggaley and Duck, 1976). Such
knowledge can be used in a double-edged way, enhanc-
ing either positive or negative tendencies in society,
according to the ideological standpoint of the person
shaping the message or programme.

As the chapter headings in this book show, the
processes of persuasion can be related to: (i) the
ways in which man learns and thus apprehends (epis-
temology); (ii) the ways in which he retains this
knowledge (memory); (iii) the reasons or purposes
which determine his actions (motivation); (iv) the
codes of communication (semiology); (v) the forms
that society takes, or to which it aspires (ideology).
These are extensive sinews. The importance given to
any one would reflect the bias or standpoint of the
person making a decision about their relative values.
We shall be content to note here that man's mental
framework, cognitive and emotive, reflects his individual traits and social conditioning, and that they
are not mutually exclusive. In fact, man as a symbol-
using creature shows quite clearly the interdependence
of inner and outer conditions; he thinks with symbols
(personal), and he communicates with symbols (social).

The literature on persuasion shows how interpretations of the subject come to be couched in terms
borrowed from theorising in other areas. For instance,
in the 1950's and 1960's (Sargant, 1957; Packard,
1962; Brown, 1963), Freudian and Pavlovian theorising
presented unique frameworks for the interpretation of
persuasion. But in more recent times (Williamson,
1978) we can notice the adoption of Lacan's ideas,
which are based jointly in psychoanalysis and linguistics. Throughout this book, there is no set
model or single theoretical concept; instead the
reader has been faced with key issues from different
discipline areas.

Because life is lived in a matrix of interactions,
critical persuasive influences may be difficult to
detect. Except for the effects of single episodes
in experimental situations, or of closed, coercive
situations where control can be systematically applied,
it is not easy to disentangle the interacting variables.
Any one response may well be the culmination of a
series of influences.

The application of learning theory to persuasion brings out the relevance of conditioning as a means for shaping particular forms of behaviour, the persuasive element being the type of reinforcement, or, more particularly, the expectation of a particular type of reinforcement. It is based mainly on events in the individual's past determining his current actions But man can not only look backward, he can also look forward to changed future conditions; he can imagine things being different. Through imagination he can create an illusion of 'how things might be', it is a condition of prospection, as distinct from the retrospection of conditioning. The following illustration (Fig. 14.1) brings out this duality:

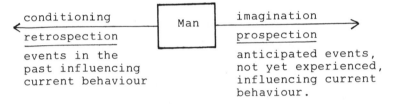

Fig. 14.1 Retrospection and Prospection.

Although the diagram separates the two conditions, the issue is not quite clear cut, because imagination uses, as its raw material, events or experiences from the past for making projections about the future. The ability of man to imagine, to project, and to conceive of himself as otherwise has strong motivational properties, hence the reason why so much of advertising and propaganda attempts to tap the energy contained therein. It is the stuff of dreams, of ideologies, and of man's desire for transformation. A mental transformation of a symbolic kind in which the persuader can implant particular meanings or connotations, and thus, if he is successful, induce the recipient to view the world from his perspective. Imagination, however, is likely to be tempered by experience; this explains why explicit and implicit appeals to the imagination of reader, viewer or listener may find limited responses of the kind desired by an advertiser; a rise in desire elicited by an advertisement may provide temporary arousal, but not lead to action; for example, a viewer may enjoy the experience of watching a particular advertisement and be temporarily aroused, but not moved to take any overt action. As stated earlier, what we need to know are the cumulative effects from the many sources of influence which bear down upon the individual.

Of the various concepts, which have been discussed in this book, that of 'meaning' is central to our understanding of persuasion. Whoever sets out to influence or persuade, whether the purpose be educational, commercial or political, he must know something about the codes of the recipients, or to use MacKay's (1969) terms, their conditional states of readiness. In communication theory terms, the sender and receiver must share a common code. Not only that, the concepts used in the message should be able to anchor themselves to concepts already existing in the cognitive frameworks of the recipients. It is not sufficient for information, whether it be persuasive in intent or otherwise, to be arousing, it must also be in a form, codewise and conceptwise, which can be processed by the recipient. Therefore, of the three types of meaning: (i) meaning to the sender; (ii) meaning to the receiver; (iii) conventional meaning; it is the second of these three conditions that determines behavioural outcomes. The first condition relates to the origin, and the third to a statistical property or norm, the level at which mass persuasion has its raison d'être. In appeals to the so-called mass, language and concepts tend to be couched in terms of the lowest common denominator. So it is that we find political orators using 'the language of the people'. Of course, when an audience is selective, either through interest, education or professional expertise, then the language of communication can be more restricted, reflecting the codes and concepts already established in its individual members.

The unpredictability of codes when viewed in the context of mass communications is of critical importance to persuasion. As Eco (1977) pointed out, sometimes the addressee's entire system of cultural references, as well as the concrete circumstances in which he lives, produce an interpretation that the sender would not have envisaged. The kind of phenomenon known in the sociology of mass communications as the 'boomerang effect', or the 'two-step flow' in which information from the sender to the addressee is filtered through opinion leaders. Because of the unpredictability of decoding, the original message may be read at a different level to the one intended. The same applies in relation to connotation; different connotations from those envisaged by the sender can arise when his cultural and experiential background is different from that

of the addressee. This is one reason why most advertisements are explicit, with meanings clearly defined;
they set out to avoid connotative proliferation when
this leads away from the intended inference.

We have seen that the study of codes and their
usage is of particular importance to persuasion; that
is, language as a code and the other semiological
conventions, such as the shaping and presentation of
pictorial images in the various media. We further
noticed that it is in the context of society that
codes are established and maintained. The history
of a society bears upon its members, and in so doing
it shapes the way in which they perceive themselves
and others. Not only that, we noticed the power
residing in the group to influence its constituent
members. Of all the various possible sources of
influence, perhaps that of the group is the most
potent. The desire for affiliation, even at the
cost of conformity to group norms, imposes strong
pressures upon the individual, and these pressures
can be considered as forms of persuasion. It is here,
at the face-to-face level, where actions can be monitored and views questioned, that individuals are
most prone to suggestion. At the level of 'distant'
persuasion through the press and television, the
individual is protected by his anonymity; he is not
asked to decide and make public his decisions or
commitments. In the group, the individual is generally compelled into declaring his position, even
silence itself can be expressive of a position. So
it appears that it is towards the group, which stands
between the individual and society at large, that we
should look for the most powerful sources of persuasion. Studies of coercive persuasion, such as those
by Schein et al (1961), highlight the importance of
the group. And we have the evidence of military
organisations, structured in a way which enhances
group solidarity, to show the importance of the
group for influencing behaviour. Group membership
implies some loss of personal identity; this being
so, we can assume that social needs may, at times,
take preference over psychological needs. And it is
this need for affiliation which lies at the base of
those advertising campaigns which stress belonging,
acceptance and togetherness. The greater the autonomy
of the individual the greater is the likelihood that
he will be able to resist such blandishments.

Of the various concepts dealt with in this book,
there is one which can be found in most of the separate themes or chapters, namely relationship. And,
on reflection, we can see that the persuader's task

is generally one of establishing relationships or of
strengthening relationships; such relationships may
be cognitive, affective or social. We can also see
that the framing of messages, be they literary or
pictorial, is a task of ordering particular relationships, putting things into particular contexts which
suggest particular meanings. For example, let us
take learning; the essence of learning is the establishment of relationships; this is so whether learning is conditioned in the Pavlovian sense, or cognitive. Learning takes place when relationships, sometimes referred to as associations or connections,
are made, without such activity there is no change
and hence no learning. We can also see that imagination rests upon the mental construction of relationships, the putting together of previously distinct images, either in new contexts or new forms,
or both. Advertisements which proffer images provide
material for the imagination to construct personal
interpretations, but in a direction which is partly
pre-formed; in other words, the individual closes
the gap in a given structure, the essence of structures being the relationship of their parts.

We also found that memory is strengthened by
relationships; when incoming information cannot find
a connection it finds difficulty in integration, i.e.
to the existing structure. In such a condition,
information tends not to be stable for any length of
time, hence it is forgotten. In order to establish
cognitive relationships, information needs to be related to that already existing, and preferably given
as many links as possible; for it to be strengthened,
it needs to be repeated.

A further example of the importance of relationships can be found in the use of metaphors as persuasive devices. Metaphors only possess meaning
when the receiver is able to make the intended link
with the absent meaning. The same applies to myths
and rituals; it is in the context of absent, or other
meaning that their signification lies; when the link
or relationship with the absent or hidden meaning is
not made, symbolic signification degenerates to a
stimulus-response condition or to one of meaningless-
ness.

The concept of relationship is also at the core
of semiology; as we saw earlier, it is the forging
of relationships between signifier and signified,
resulting in the sign, which creates the conditions
for connotation. We can see that media manipulation
also is a task of shaping relationships: relationships
in the material form of the media,pictures,illustrations

text; the juxtaposition of text to advertisements.
Such manipulations may result from the demands of
the media as artefacts, or from deliberate intention
to produce a desired effect. We can extend the relationship concept further to include group influence.
The involvement in groups implies that the individual
member puts himself into a particular kind of relationship, i.e. to other people, which helps to determine or influence his behaviour or attitude.

Through the concept of relationship, which is
tacitly present throughout much of this book, we can
discern the most significant connection with communication theory. Although, admittedly, persuasion
cannot exist without communication (here we refer to
the variety of expressive acts which man has at his
disposal), the major difference lies in intent.
Communication can be studied without invoking the
concept of intent, but persuasion cannot. Because
intent is central to persuasion we are faced with the
issue of value judgements, thus the problem of persuasion is one which requires ethical resolution, a.
resolution which would be misleading should it fail
to take into account both intent and context.

REFERENCES

BAGGALEY, J. and DUCK, S. (1976) _Dynamics of
    Television._ Farnborough, Hants: Saxon House.
BALFOUR, M. (1979) _Propaganda in War 1939-1945._
    London: Routledge.
BROWN, J.A.C. (1963) _Techniques of Persuasion._
    Harmondsworth: Penguin.
CRUICKSHANK, C. (1977) _The Fourth Arm: Psychological
    Warfare 1938-1945._ London: Davis-Poynter.
ECO, U. (1977) _A Theory of Semiotics._ London:
    Macmillan.
HOVLAND, C.I. (ed.) (1957) _The Order of Presentation
    in Persuasion._ New Haven: Yale University Press.
MacKAY, D.M. (1969) _Information, Mechanism and
    Meaning._ Cambridge, Mass.: M.I.T. Press.
PACKARD, V. (1962) _The Hidden Persuaders._
    Harmondsworth: Penguin.
SARGANT, W. (1957) _Battle for the Mind._ London:
    Heinemann.
SCHEIN, E.H., SCHNEIER, I. and BARKER, C.H. (1961)
    Coercive Persuasion. New York: W.W. Norton & Co.
WILLIAMSON, J. (1978) _Decoding Advertisements._
    London: Marion Boyars.

Index

Index

Index